# bbq
# food

# bbq
# food

Kay Scarlett

LAUREL
GLEN

San Diego, California

# Contents

Skewers     6

Burgers     44

Entrées     72

Sides     294

Desserts     364

Basics     386

Index     394

# Skewers

## Pork skewers in green ginger wine and soy marinade with grilled scallions

1 lb. 12 oz. pork fillets, trimmed
1 tablespoon finely grated fresh
   ginger
2 garlic cloves, finely chopped
1 tablespoon finely chopped
   preserved ginger in syrup
1/4 cup green ginger wine (see Note)
2 1/2 tablespoons kecap manis
1/2 teaspoon sesame oil
1 tablespoon vegetable oil
8 scallions, green parts removed,
   quartered
1 tablespoon olive oil
fresh cilantro

Cut the pork into 5 x 1-inch strips and put them in a nonmetallic bowl with the ginger, garlic, preserved ginger, green ginger wine, kecap manis, and oils, turning the meat to make sure it is evenly coated. Cover and refrigerate the bowl and leave it to marinate for at least 2 hours or overnight. Soak twelve wooden skewers in cold water for 1 hour, then thread four pork strips into an S-shape onto each skewer. Cover the skewers and refrigerate until you are ready to start cooking.

Preheat the barbecue to medium direct heat. Toss the scallions with the olive oil and season with salt and freshly ground black pepper. Cook them on the flat plate for 10 minutes or until they are softened and well browned. When the scallions are nearly cooked, put the kebabs on the grill and grill them for 2 minutes on each side or until the pork is just cooked through and glazed. Garnish the skewers with cilantro and serve immediately with the scallions.

Serves 4

Note: Green ginger wine is a sweet, fortified wine with a distinctive ginger flavor. It originated in Britain.

## Beef kebabs with mint yogurt dressing

2 lb. 4 oz. lean beef fillet, cubed
1/2 cup olive oil
1/3 cup lemon juice
1 tablespoon chopped rosemary
2 small red onions, cut into wedges
7 oz. slender eggplants, sliced

*Mint yogurt dressing*
1 cup plain yogurt
1 garlic clove, crushed
1 small cucumber, grated
2 tablespoons chopped mint

Put the beef in a nonmetallic bowl. Combine the olive oil, lemon juice, and rosemary and pour over the beef. Cover and refrigerate for 2 hours.

To make the mint yogurt dressing, mix together the yogurt, garlic, cucumber, and mint and season with salt and pepper.

Drain the beef and thread onto long metallic skewers, alternating pieces of beef with the onion wedges and slices of eggplant.

Cook the kebabs on a hot, lightly oiled barbecue grill or grill pan, turning often, for 5–10 minutes or until the beef is cooked through and tender. Serve with the dressing.

Makes 8 kebabs

# Tofu kebabs with miso pesto

1 large red pepper, cubed
12 button mushrooms, halved
6 pickled onions, quartered
3 zucchini, cut into chunks
1 lb. firm tofu, cubed
½ cup light olive oil
3 tablespoons light soy sauce
2 garlic cloves, crushed
2 teaspoons grated fresh ginger

*Miso pesto*
½ cup unsalted roasted peanuts
2 cups cilantro leaves
2 tablespoons white miso paste
2 garlic cloves
scant ½ cup olive oil

If using wooden skewers, soak them in water for 30 minutes to prevent scorching. Thread the vegetables and tofu alternately onto twelve skewers, then place in a large nonmetallic dish.

Mix together the olive oil, soy sauce, garlic, and ginger, then pour half over the kebabs. Cover and leave to marinate for 1 hour.

To make the miso pesto, finely chop the peanuts, cilantro, miso paste, and garlic in a food processor. Slowly add the olive oil while the machine is still running and blend to a smooth paste.

Cook the kebabs on a hot, lightly oiled barbecue flat plate or grill, turning and brushing with the remaining marinade, for 4–6 minutes or until the edges are slightly brown. Serve with the miso pesto.

Serves 4

# Garlic and mint lamb skewers with almond couscous and yogurt sauce

8 lamb fillets, trimmed and cut
into 1-inch cubes
2 tablespoons olive oil
1/3 cup lemon juice
2 garlic cloves, crushed
2 teaspoons dried mint leaves

*Yogurt sauce*
1 cup thick yogurt
1 garlic clove, crushed

*Almond couscous*
2 cups instant couscous
1 tablespoon olive oil
2 cups chicken stock
3 tablespoons butter
2 teaspoons ras el hanout (if you
are unable to find it, see page 83
for a recipe to make your own)
1/4 cup currants, soaked in warm
water for 10 minutes
1/2 cup slivered almonds, toasted
1/2 cup chopped mint leaves

Put the lamb in a nonmetallic bowl with the olive oil, lemon juice, garlic, and mint. Stir the pieces around until well coated and season with black pepper. Cover and refrigerate for at least 4 hours or overnight.

Make the yogurt sauce by mixing the yogurt and garlic in a small bowl, then refrigerate it until you are ready to use it.

Put the couscous in a heatproof bowl, drizzle it with the olive oil, and season well with salt. Bring the chicken stock to a boil and pour it over the couscous, then cover the bowl and leave it for 10 minutes to absorb the stock. Add the butter and fluff it through with a fork until it has melted and the grains are separated. Stir in the ras el hanout, currants, almonds, and mint and season to taste with salt and pepper.

Soak eight wooden skewers in cold water for 1 hour, then thread the lamb onto them and season well. Preheat the barbecue to medium–high direct heat and grill the skewers for about 3–4 minutes on each side or until they are cooked to your liking. Serve the skewers on a bed of couscous with the yogurt sauce.

Serves 4

# Involtini of swordfish

2 lb. 4 oz. swordfish, skin removed,
    cut into four 2-inch pieces
3 lemons
⅓ cup olive oil
1 small onion, chopped
3 garlic cloves, chopped
2 tablespoons chopped capers
2 tablespoons chopped pitted
    kalamata olives
⅓ cup finely grated Parmesan cheese
1½ cups fresh bread crumbs
2 tablespoons chopped parsley
1 egg, lightly beaten
24 fresh bay leaves
2 small white onions, quartered and
    separated into pieces
2 tablespoons lemon juice, extra

Cut each swordfish piece horizontally into four slices to give you sixteen slices in total. Place each piece between two pieces of plastic wrap and roll gently with a rolling pin to flatten without tearing. Cut each piece in half to make thirty-two pieces.

Peel the lemons with a vegetable peeler. Cut the peel into twenty-four even pieces. Squeeze the lemons to produce 3 tablespoons of juice.

Heat 2 tablespoons olive oil in a pan, add the onion and garlic, and cook over medium heat for 2 minutes. Place in a bowl with the capers, olives, Parmesan, bread crumbs, and parsley. Season, add the egg, and mix to bind.

Divide the stuffing among the fish pieces and, with oiled hands, roll up to form pockets. Thread four rolls onto each of eight skewers, alternating with the bay leaves, lemon peel, and onion.

Mix the remaining oil with the lemon juice in a bowl. Cook the skewers on a hot grill for 3–4 minutes on each side, basting with the oil and lemon mixture. Serve with a little extra lemon juice drizzled over the top.

Serves 4

## Sweet-and-sour pork kebabs

2 lb. 4 oz. pork fillets, cubed
1 large red pepper, cubed
1 large green pepper, cubed
15-oz. can pineapple pieces, drained,
    juice reserved
1 cup orange juice
3 tablespoons white vinegar
2 tablespoons brown sugar
2 teaspoons chili garlic sauce
2 teaspoons cornstarch

Soak wooden skewers in water for 30 minutes to prevent scorching. Thread pieces of meat alternately with pieces of pepper and pineapple onto the skewers. Mix the pineapple juice with the orange juice, vinegar, sugar, and sauce. Place the kebabs in a shallow nonmetallic dish and pour half the marinade over them. Cover and refrigerate for at least 3 hours, turning occasionally.

Put the remaining marinade in a small saucepan. Mix the cornstarch with 1 tablespoon of the marinade until smooth, then add to the pan. Stir over medium heat until the mixture boils and thickens. Transfer to a bowl, cover the surface with plastic wrap, and leave to cool.

Cook the kebabs on a hot, lightly oiled flat plate or grill for 15 minutes, turning occasionally, until tender. Serve with the sauce.

Serves 6

## Satay chicken

1 lb. 2 oz. chicken thigh fillets, cut
  into 1/2-inch-wide strips
1 garlic clove, crushed
2 teaspoons finely grated fresh ginger
3 teaspoons fish sauce

*Satay sauce*
2 teaspoons peanut oil
4 red Asian shallots, finely chopped
4 garlic cloves, crushed
2 teaspoons finely chopped fresh
  ginger
2 small red chilies, seeded and finely
  chopped
1/2 cup crunchy peanut butter
1 3/4 cups coconut milk
2 teaspoons soy sauce
2 teaspoons brown sugar
1 1/2 tablespoons fish sauce
1 fresh kaffir lime leaf
1 1/2 tablespoons lime juice

Put the chicken, garlic, ginger, and
fish sauce in a bowl and turn the
chicken so that it is well coated.
Cover the bowl and leave it in the
refrigerator for 1 hour. Soak twelve
wooden skewers in cold water for
1 hour.

To make the satay sauce, heat the
oil in a saucepan over medium heat,
then add the shallots, garlic, ginger,
and chilies. Stir the mixture constantly
with a wooden spoon for 5 minutes or
until the shallots are golden. Reduce
the heat to low, add the remaining
sauce ingredients, and simmer for
10 minutes or until the sauce has
thickened. Remove the lime leaf and
keep the sauce warm while you cook
the chicken.

Preheat the barbecue grill to medium–
high. Thread two or three chicken
strips onto each skewer without
crowding them and grill the chicken
for 10 minutes or until it is cooked
through, turning after 5 minutes.
Serve the skewers with the satay
sauce. Delicious with cucumber salad
(see page 350).

Serves 4

# Scallop and fish rosemary skewers with marjoram dressing and grilled radicchio salad

2 tablespoons marjoram leaves
1 tablespoon lemon juice
1/3 cup olive oil, plus extra for brushing
1/4 cup chopped Italian parsley
8 long, firm rosemary branches
1 lb. 5 oz. firm white fish fillets, cut
    into 1 1/4-inch cubes
16 scallops with roe attached
2 heads radicchio, green outer leaves
    removed, cut into 8 wedges
1 3/4 oz. arugula leaves
lemon wedges

Pound the marjoram leaves in a mortar and pestle with a little salt, or chop them very finely until they become a paste. Add the lemon juice, then stir in the olive oil and parsley and season to taste.

Pull the leaves off the rosemary branches, leaving just a tuft at the end of each stem. Thread three pieces of fish and two scallops alternately onto each rosemary skewer, brush them with a little olive oil, and season well.

Preheat the barbecue flat plate to medium direct heat. Cook the skewers for 3–4 minutes on each side or until the fish is cooked through. While the skewers are cooking, add the radicchio to the plate in batches for 1–2 minutes on each side or until it is just wilted and slightly browned. Put the radicchio wedges on a tray in a single layer so that the leaves don't steam in their own heat.

Arrange the radicchio on a flat serving dish, gently combine it with the arugula, and drizzle a little of the marjoram dressing on top. Serve the skewers with the radicchio salad, lemon wedges, and extra dressing.

Serves 4

# Paprika lamb kebabs with skordalia

2 lb. 4 oz. lamb sirloin, cut into
   3/4-inch cubes
1 tablespoon sweet paprika
1 tablespoon hot paprika
1/2 cup lemon juice
1/2 cup olive oil
3 large floury potatoes (e.g., russet),
   cut into large cubes
3–4 garlic cloves, crushed with a
   pinch of salt
10 1/2 oz. spinach leaves
lemon wedges, to serve

Thread six lamb cubes onto metallic skewers, then place in a nonmetallic dish. Combine both the paprikas, 1/3 cup lemon juice, and 1/4 cup oil in a nonmetallic pitcher. Pour over the skewers, turning to coat well. Season with pepper. Cover and chill while making the skordalia.

Boil the potatoes for 20 minutes or until tender. Drain and place the potatoes, garlic, and 1 tablespoon of the lemon juice in a food processor. With the motor running, slowly add the remaining oil in a thin stream and blend for 30–60 seconds or until all the oil is incorporated—avoid overprocessing, as it will become gluey. Season to taste, then set aside to serve at room temperature.

Preheat a barbecue grill and brush with oil. Grill the skewers for 3–4 minutes each side for medium-rare or 5–6 minutes for well done.

Wash the spinach and add to a saucepan with just a little water clinging to the leaves. Cook, covered, over medium heat for 1–2 minutes or until wilted. Remove from the heat and stir in the remaining lemon juice. Serve the kebabs immediately with the skordalia, spinach, and lemon wedges.

Serves 4

# Tuna skewers with Moroccan spices and chermoula

1 lb. 12 oz. tuna steaks, cut
    into cubes
2 tablespoons olive oil
1/2 teaspoon ground cumin
2 teaspoons grated lemon zest
couscous, to serve

*Chermoula*
3 teaspoons ground cumin
1/2 teaspoon ground coriander
2 teaspoons paprika
pinch of cayenne pepper
4 garlic cloves, crushed
1/2 cup chopped Italian parsley
1/2 cup chopped cilantro
1/3 cup lemon juice
1/2 cup olive oil

If using wooden skewers, soak for 30 minutes beforehand to prevent scorching. Place the tuna in a shallow nonmetallic dish. Combine the olive oil, ground cumin, and lemon zest and pour over the tuna. Toss to coat and leave to marinate for 10 minutes.

To make the chermoula, place the cumin, coriander, paprika, and cayenne pepper in a frying pan and cook over medium heat for 30 seconds or until fragrant. Combine with the remaining ingredients and leave for the flavors to develop.

Thread the tuna onto the skewers. Cook on a hot, lightly oiled barbecue grill or flat plate until cooked to your liking (about 1 minute on each side for rare and 2 minutes for medium). Serve on couscous with the chermoula drizzled over the skewers.

Serves 4

# Spice-rubbed pork kebabs with garlic sauce

1 lb. 12 oz. pork neck fillets, trimmed
2 teaspoons fennel seeds
2 teaspoons coriander seeds
1 tablespoon olive oil

*Garlic sauce*
4 garlic cloves, coarsely chopped
1 thick slice of white bread, crusts
   removed
1/4 cup olive oil
1 1/2 tablespoons lemon juice

lemon wedges, to serve
pita bread, to serve

Soak eight wooden skewers in cold water for 1 hour and cut the pork into ³/₄-inch cubes. Dry-fry the fennel and coriander seeds for about 30 seconds or until they are fragrant, then grind them in a spice grinder or mortar and pestle. Mix the ground spices with the olive oil and toss the pork in it until the meat is well coated. Cover and refrigerate for 2 hours.

To make the garlic sauce, crush the garlic cloves in a mortar and pestle with ¹/₂ teaspoon salt until you have a very smooth paste. Tear the bread into pieces and leave it in a bowl with enough warm water to cover it. Let it soak for 5 minutes, then squeeze out the bread and add it to the garlic a little at a time, pounding as you go, until you have a smooth paste. Keep pounding as you add the olive oil, 1 tablespoon at a time, until it has all been added, then add 3 tablespoons of boiling water, 1 tablespoon at a time, and stir in the lemon juice. You should end up with a smooth, thick paste.

Thread the pork onto the soaked skewers and season the kebabs well with salt and ground pepper. Preheat the barbecue grill to medium–high and grill the kebabs for 10 minutes or until they are cooked through, turning them halfway through the cooking time. Drizzle the kebabs with a little garlic sauce and put the rest of the sauce in a small bowl to serve at the table. Serve with the lemon wedges and warm pita bread. The fennel salad (see page 309) makes a delicious accompaniment.

Serves 4

Note: You can also use a small food processor to make the garlic sauce. Beware! It has a very strong flavor, so only a little is needed.

# Persian chicken skewers

2 teaspoons ground cardamom
1/2 teaspoon ground turmeric
1 teaspoon ground allspice
4 garlic cloves, crushed
1/4 cup lemon juice
1/4 cup olive oil
4 large chicken thigh fillets,
   excess fat removed
lemon wedges, to serve
plain yogurt, to serve

To make the marinade, whisk together the cardamom, turmeric, allspice, garlic, lemon juice, and oil. Season with salt and ground black pepper.

Cut the chicken thigh fillets into 1 1/2-inch cubes. Toss the cubes in the spice marinade. Cover and refrigerate overnight.

Thread the chicken onto metal skewers and cook on a hot, lightly oiled barbecue grill or flat plate for 4 minutes on each side or until the chicken is cooked through. Serve with lemon wedges and plain yogurt.

Serves 4

## Skewered lamb with chili aioli

3 lb. 5 oz. leg of lamb, boned
  and cubed
1/2 cup olive oil
1/2 cup lemon juice
2 garlic cloves, crushed
1 teaspoon cracked black pepper
1 tablespoon Dijon mustard
1 tablespoon chopped oregano

*Chili aioli*
2–3 small red chilies, seeded
3 garlic cloves
1/2 teaspoon ground black pepper
3 egg yolks
2 tablespoons lemon juice
scant 1 cup olive oil

Put the lamb in a large nonmetallic bowl. Add the combined olive oil, lemon juice, garlic, pepper, mustard, and oregano. Toss well, cover, and refrigerate for at least 3 hours.

Soak twelve wooden skewers in water to prevent scorching. Drain the lamb, reserving the marinade. Thread the lamb onto the skewers and cook on a hot, lightly oiled barbecue grill or flat plate until well browned, brushing with the marinade occasionally.

To make the chili aioli, chop the chilies and garlic for 30 seconds in a food processor. Add the pepper, egg yolks, and 2 teaspoons lemon juice. With the motor running, slowly pour in the oil in a fine stream. Increase the flow as the aioli thickens. Add the remaining lemon juice and season to taste. Serve with the skewered lamb.

Makes 12 skewers

## Mushroom and eggplant skewers with tomato sauce

12 long rosemary sprigs
18 portobello mushrooms, halved
1 small eggplant, cubed
1/4 cup olive oil
2 tablespoons balsamic vinegar
2 garlic cloves, crushed
1 teaspoon sugar

*Tomato sauce*
5 tomatoes
1 tablespoon olive oil
1 small onion, finely chopped
1 garlic clove, crushed
1 tablespoon tomato paste
2 teaspoons sugar
2 teaspoons balsamic vinegar
1 tablespoon chopped Italian parsley

Remove the leaves from the lower part of the rosemary sprigs. Reserve 1 tablespoon of the leaves. Put the mushrooms and eggplant in a large nonmetallic bowl. Pour in the combined oil, vinegar, garlic, and sugar and toss. Marinate for about 15 minutes.

To make the tomato sauce, score a cross in the base of each tomato. Put in a bowl of boiling water for 30 seconds, then plunge into cold water. Peel the skin away from the cross. Cut in half and scoop out the seeds with a spoon. Dice the flesh.

Heat the oil in a saucepan. Cook the onion and garlic over medium heat for 2–3 minutes or until soft. Reduce the heat. Add the tomato, tomato paste, sugar, vinegar, and parsley and simmer for 10 minutes or until thick.

Carefully thread alternating mushroom halves and eggplant cubes onto the rosemary sprigs. Cook on a hot, lightly oiled barbecue grill or flat plate for 7–8 minutes or until the eggplant is tender, turning occasionally. Serve with the sauce.

Serves 4

# Vegetarian skewers with basil couscous

5 thin zucchini, cut into ³/₄-inch cubes
5 slender eggplants, cut into ³/₄-inch cubes
12 button mushrooms, halved
2 red peppers, cut into ³/₄-inch cubes
9 oz. kefalotiri cheese, cut into ³/₄-inch-thick pieces
¹/₃ cup lemon juice
2 garlic cloves, finely chopped
5 tablespoons finely chopped basil
¹/₂ cup plus 2 tablespoons extra-virgin olive oil
1 cup couscous
1 teaspoon grated lemon zest
lemon wedges, to serve

Using twelve metallic skewers, thread pieces of vegetables and kefalotiri alternately, starting and finishing with pepper and using two pieces of kefalotiri per skewer. Place in a large nonmetallic dish. Combine the lemon juice, garlic, 4 tablespoons basil, and ¹/₂ cup of oil in a nonmetallic bowl. Season. Pour two-thirds of the marinade over the skewers, reserving the remainder. Turn the skewers to coat evenly, cover with plastic wrap, and marinate for at least 5 minutes.

Put the couscous, zest, and 1¹/₂ cups boiling water in a large heatproof bowl. Let stand for 5 minutes or until the water has been absorbed. Add the remaining 2 tablespoons oil and the basil, then fluff with a fork to separate the grains.

Meanwhile, heat a barbecue plate to medium–high. Cook the skewers, brushing often with the leftover marinade, for 4–5 minutes each side or until the vegetables are cooked and the cheese browns.

Divide the couscous and skewers among four serving plates. Season, then drizzle with the reserved marinade. Serve immediately with lemon wedges.

Serves 4

## Salmon and shrimp kebabs with Chinese spices

7 oz. salmon fillets
36 raw shrimp, peeled and deveined,
    tails intact
2-inch piece fresh ginger, finely
    shredded
$2/3$ cup Chinese rice wine
$3/4$ cup kecap manis
$1/2$ teaspoon five-spice powder
7 oz. fresh egg noodles
1 lb. 5 oz. baby bok choy, leaves
    separated

Remove the skin and bones from the salmon and cut it into bite-size cubes (you should have about thirty-six). Thread three cubes of salmon alternately with three shrimp onto each skewer. Lay the skewers in a nonmetallic dish.

Mix together the ginger, rice wine, kecap manis, and five-spice powder. Pour over the skewers, then cover and marinate for at least 2 hours. Turn over a few times to ensure even coating.

Drain, reserving the marinade. Cook the skewers in batches on a hot, lightly oiled barbecue flat plate or grill for 4–5 minutes each side or until they are cooked through.

Meanwhile, place the noodles in a bowl and cover with boiling water. Leave for 5 minutes or until tender, then drain and keep warm. Place the reserved marinade in a saucepan and bring to a boil. Reduce the heat, simmer, and stir in the bok choy leaves. Cook, covered, for 2 minutes or until just wilted.

Top the noodles with the bok choy, then the kebabs. Spoon the heated marinade on top, season, and serve.

Serves 4

## Mediterranean chicken skewers

2 large chicken breast fillets, cut
  into 32 cubes
24 cherry tomatoes
6 porcini mushrooms, cut into
  quarters
2 garlic cloves, crushed
zest of 1 lemon, grated
2 tablespoons lemon juice
2 tablespoons olive oil
1 tablespoon oregano leaves,
  chopped

Soak eight wooden skewers in water to prevent scorching. Thread a piece of chicken onto each skewer, followed by a tomato, then a piece of mushroom. Repeat twice for each skewer and finish with a piece of chicken. Put the skewers in a shallow nonmetallic dish.

Combine the garlic, lemon zest, lemon juice, olive oil, and chopped oregano, pour over the skewers, and toss well. Marinate for at least 2 hours, or overnight if time permits.

Cook the skewers on a hot, lightly oiled barbecue grill or flat plate for 4 minutes on each side, basting occasionally, until the chicken is cooked and the tomatoes have shriveled slightly.

Makes 8 skewers

# Burgers

## Chili beef burgers

1 lb. 2 oz. ground beef
6 red Asian shallots, finely chopped
1/4 cup crisp fried onion flakes
   (see Note)
3 garlic cloves, finely chopped
2 long red chilies, seeded and finely
   chopped
1/3 cup finely chopped cilantro leaves
   (include some stems)
2–2 1/2 tablespoons chili garlic sauce
   (see Note)
1 egg, lightly beaten
2 cups fresh bread crumbs

olive oil, for brushing
1 loaf Turkish bread, cut into 4 pieces,
   or 4 round Turkish rolls
3 handfuls mignonette or green oak
   lettuce leaves

To make the burgers, put the beef, shallots, onion flakes, garlic, chili, cilantro, chili garlic sauce, egg, bread crumbs, and 1 1/2 teaspoons of salt in a large bowl and knead well with your hands until the ingredients are thoroughly combined. Cover the bowl and refrigerate for 2 hours.

Using wet hands, divide the beef mixture into four equal portions, roll each portion into a ball, then flatten it slightly to form patties. Preheat the grill to medium direct heat. Brush the patties lightly with oil and grill them for 5–6 minutes, then flip them over and cook for another 5–6 minutes or until they are well browned and cooked through. A few minutes before the patties are done, toast the bread, cut-side down, on the grill for 1–2 minutes or until it is marked and golden.

Divide the lettuce among four of the toasted bread slices. Add a patty, season the burgers with salt and pepper, then top with the remaining toasted bread. Delicious served with pineapple mint salsa (see page 318).

Serves 4

Note: Crisp fried onion flakes and chili garlic sauce are available from Asian markets.

# Tuna burgers with herbed mayonnaise

4 garlic cloves, crushed
2 egg yolks
1 cup light olive oil
3 tablespoons chopped Italian parsley
1 tablespoon chopped dill
2 teaspoons Dijon mustard
1 tablespoon lemon juice
1 tablespoon red wine vinegar
1 tablespoon baby capers in brine, drained
4 anchovy fillets in oil, drained
4 tuna steaks, 5$\frac{1}{2}$ oz. each
2 tablespoons olive oil
2 red onions, thinly sliced
4 large round bread rolls, halved and buttered
3$\frac{1}{2}$ oz. mixed lettuce leaves

Put the garlic and egg yolks in a food processor and process them together for 10 seconds. With the motor running, add the oil in a very thin, slow stream. When the mixture starts to thicken, start pouring the oil a little faster until all of the oil has been added and the mixture is thick and creamy. Add the parsley, dill, mustard, lemon juice, vinegar, capers, and anchovies and process until the mixture is smooth. Refrigerate the mayonnaise until you need it.

Preheat the grill to high. Brush the tuna steaks with 1 tablespoon of olive oil and cook them for 2 minutes on each side or until they are almost cooked through. Add the remaining olive oil to the onion, toss to separate and coat the rings, and cook on the flat plate for 2 minutes or until the onion is soft and caramelized. Toast the rolls, buttered-side down, on the grill for 1 minute or until they are marked and golden.

Put some lettuce, a tuna steak, some of the onion, and a dollop of herbed mayonnaise on one half of each roll. Season with salt and pepper and top with the other half of the roll.

Serves 4

## Pork and tomato burgers

12 oz. ground pork and veal
½ cup sun-dried tomatoes, chopped
3 scallions, finely chopped
2 tablespoons chopped basil
1 red pepper, seeded and sliced
olive oil, for cooking
1 tablespoon balsamic vinegar

Mix together the pork and veal, sun-dried tomatoes, scallions, and basil. Season well and knead for 2 minutes or until a little sticky. Form into four patties and refrigerate for at least 15 minutes.

Mix the red pepper with a little olive oil. Cook on a hot, lightly oiled barbecue grill or flat plate, tossing well and drizzling with the balsamic vinegar, until just softened. Set aside.

Wipe the barbecue clean and reheat. Brush the burgers with a little olive oil and cook for 4–5 minutes each side or until browned and cooked through. Serve with the grilled red pepper.

Serves 4

## Yakitori chicken burgers

4 chicken thigh fillets, trimmed
3/4 cup yakitori sauce
1 teaspoon cornstarch
vegetable oil, for brushing
4 soft hamburger buns, halved
1/3 cup Japanese mayonnaise
  (see Note)
2 handfuls mizuna lettuce
1 cucumber, ends trimmed and
  shaved into ribbons with a
  vegetable peeler

Toss the chicken and yakitori sauce together in a bowl until the chicken fillets are well coated, then cover and refrigerate for 4 hours.

Drain the yakitori sauce from the chicken into a small saucepan and sprinkle it with the cornstarch. Stir the cornstarch into the marinade, bring the mixture to a boil, and simmer, stirring frequently, for 5 minutes or until it is thickened, then keep it warm.

Lightly brush the grill with oil, preheat it to low–medium heat, and cook the chicken on the grill for 6–7 minutes on each side or until it is cooked through. Toast the hamburger buns for about 1 minute on each side or until they are marked and golden.

Spread some mayonnaise on the inside surface of each bun, cover the base with mizuna and cucumber ribbons, and top with the chicken. Spread some of the thickened marinade over the chicken and top with the other half of the bun.

Serves 4

Note: Japanese mayonnaise will be available in larger supermarkets and Asian markets. If you can't find it, use regular mayonnaise.

## Beef and mozzarella burgers with grilled tomatoes

1 lb. 2 oz. ground beef
2 cups fresh bread crumbs
1 small red onion, very finely chopped
4 garlic cloves, crushed
1/2 cup finely shredded basil leaves
1/4 cup finely chopped pitted black olives
1 tablespoon balsamic vinegar
1 egg
8 pieces mozzarella, 3/4 x 1 1/4 x 1/4 inch
olive oil spray

*Grilled tomatoes*
6 Roma tomatoes
1 1/2 tablespoons olive oil

Put the beef, bread crumbs, onion, garlic, basil, olives, balsamic vinegar, and egg in a large bowl and season well with salt and pepper. Use your hands to mix it all together, then cover and refrigerate the mixture for about 2 hours.

Divide the beef mixture into eight portions and roll each portion into a ball. Push a piece of mozzarella into the middle of each ball, then push the mixture over to cover the hole and flatten the ball to form a patty.

To make the grilled tomatoes, slice the tomatoes in half lengthwise and toss them with the olive oil. Spray the flat plate with olive oil and preheat it to high. Cook the tomatoes, cut-side down, for 8 minutes, then turn them over and cook for another 5 minutes or until they are soft.

Cook the patties on one side for 5 minutes, then flip them and cook for another 5 minutes or until they are completely cooked through and the cheese has melted. Serve the burgers and grilled tomatoes with a fresh green salad.

Serves 4

## Pork sausage burgers with mustard cream

1 lb. 12 oz. ground pork
1 small onion, finely chopped
1 cup fresh bread crumbs
2 garlic cloves, crushed
1 egg, lightly beaten
1 teaspoon dried sage
6 long bread rolls

*Mustard cream*
1/2 cup sour cream
1 tablespoon whole-grain mustard
2 teaspoons lemon juice

Mix together the pork, onion, bread crumbs, garlic, egg, and sage with your hands. Season well. Divide the mixture into six portions and shape into sausages.

Cook the sausages on a hot, lightly oiled barbecue flat plate or grill for 5–10 minutes, turning occasionally.

To make the mustard cream, put the sour cream, mustard, and juice in a small bowl and stir together. Spread each cut side of the rolls with a little mustard cream, then sandwich the sausage burgers in the middle. Serve with the remaining mustard cream.

Serves 6

## Lamb burgers

1 tablespoon ground cumin
1 cup plain yogurt
½ cucumber, grated
1 tablespoon finely chopped mint
  leaves
1 tablespoon olive oil
1 onion, finely chopped
2 garlic cloves, crushed
1 lb. 12 oz. ground lamb
2 tablespoons finely chopped
  Italian parsley
2 tablespoons finely chopped cilantro
2 red peppers, quartered and seeded
1 tablespoon olive oil, extra
2 red onions, thinly sliced
olive oil spray
1 loaf Turkish bread, cut into 4 pieces
  and split horizontally
3½ oz. baby arugula leaves

Dry-fry 1 teaspoon ground cumin over medium heat for 30 seconds or until it is fragrant. Put the yogurt, cucumber, mint, and dry-fried cumin in a small bowl and mix it all together. Cover the bowl and refrigerate until needed.

Heat the oil in a frying pan and cook the onion over medium heat for 2–3 minutes or until softened. Add the garlic and remaining cumin, cook it for another minute, then allow the mixture to cool. Put the onion mixture in a large bowl with the lamb, parsley, and cilantro, season with salt and pepper, and mix it together with your hands. Divide the mixture into four portions and shape each portion into a 3/4-inch-thick patty.

Heat the barbecue to medium–high. Toss the pepper with the extra oil and cook it on the flat plate for 6 minutes on each side or until it is softened and lightly charred. Grill the patties on the flat plate for 5–6 minutes each side or until they are done.

Spray the red onion with the olive oil spray and cook it on the flat plate for 2–3 minutes or until soft and golden. Toast the bread, cut-side down, on the grill for 1–2 minutes or until it is marked and golden.

To assemble the burgers, put some arugula on four of the bread slices. Put a patty on top, then the pepper and onion. Dollop 2–3 tablespoons of the yogurt mixture on each and season with salt and freshly ground black pepper. Top with the remaining bread slices and serve immediately.

Serves 4

## Steak sandwich with balsamic onions and sun-dried tomato and basil cream

1/2 cup sour cream
1/4 cup sun-dried tomatoes, well
  drained and finely chopped
3 garlic cloves, crushed
2 tablespoons finely chopped
  basil leaves
2 teaspoons lemon juice
2 red onions
2 tablespoons olive oil
2 tablespoons balsamic vinegar
1 tablespoon brown sugar
8 large slices sourdough bread
14-oz. piece of fillet steak, cut into
  1/2-inch-thick slices
2 oz. baby arugula leaves, rinsed
  and well drained

Preheat the barbecue to medium–high. Mix the sour cream, sun-dried tomatoes, garlic, basil, and lemon juice in a small bowl and season the mixture to taste.

Thinly slice the onions, separate the rings, and toss them with 1 tablespoon of olive oil. Spread the onion across the flat grill plate and cook it for 10 minutes or until softened and starting to brown. Gather the rings into a pile and pour the combined balsamic vinegar and sugar over them. Turn the onion so that it is well coated in the balsamic mixture, then spread it out a little and cook for a few more minutes or until it is slightly glazed. Remove the onion from the barbecue and toast the bread on the grill for 30 seconds on each side or until grill marks appear.

Brush the steaks with a little olive oil and season with salt and ground black pepper. Grill them for 1 minute each side for medium–rare or 2 minutes for well done.

To serve, put a piece of steak on a slice of toasted bread and top with the onion, a dollop of the sour cream mixture, and some arugula leaves. Finish with a second piece of toast.

Serves 4

## Vegetarian burgers with cilantro garlic cream

1 cup red lentils
1 tablespoon vegetable oil
2 onions, sliced
1 tablespoon tandoori mix powder
15-oz. can chickpeas, drained
1 tablespoon grated fresh ginger
1 egg
3 tablespoons chopped Italian parsley
2 tablespoons chopped cilantro
2¼ cups fresh bread crumbs
all-purpose flour, for dusting

*Cilantro garlic cream*
½ cup sour cream
½ cup cream
1 garlic clove, crushed
2 tablespoons chopped cilantro
2 tablespoons chopped Italian parsley

Simmer the lentils in a large pan of water for 8 minutes or until tender. Drain well. Heat the oil in a pan and cook the onion until tender. Add the tandoori mix and stir until fragrant.

Place the chickpeas, half the lentils, and the ginger, egg, and onion mixture in a food processor. Process for 20 seconds or until smooth. Transfer to a bowl. Stir in the remaining lentils, parsley, cilantro, and bread crumbs.

Divide into ten portions and shape into patties (if the mixture is too soft, refrigerate for 15 minutes to firm). Toss the patties in flour and place on a hot, lightly oiled grill or flat plate. Cook for 3–4 minutes each side or until browned.

For the cilantro garlic cream, mix together the sour cream, cream, garlic, and herbs. Serve with the burgers.

Makes 10 burgers

## Cheeseburgers with red pepper salsa

*Red pepper salsa*
2 red peppers
1 ripe tomato, finely chopped
1 small red onion, finely chopped
1 tablespoon olive oil
2 teaspoons red wine vinegar

2 lb. 4 oz. ground beef
1 small onion, finely chopped
2 tablespoons chopped Italian parsley
1 teaspoon dried oregano
1 tablespoon tomato paste
2½ oz. cheddar cheese
6 bread rolls
salad leaves, to serve

To make the salsa, quarter the peppers, remove the seeds and membranes, and cook on a hot, lightly oiled grill, skin-side down, until the skin blackens and blisters. Place in a plastic bag and leave to cool. Peel away the skin and dice the flesh. Combine with the tomato, onion, olive oil, and vinegar and leave for at least 1 hour to let the flavors develop. Serve at room temperature.

Mix together the ground beef, onion, herbs, and tomato paste with your hands and season well. Divide into six portions and shape into patties. Cut the cheese into small squares. Make a cavity in the top of each patty with your thumb. Place a piece of cheese in the cavity and smooth the ground beef over to enclose the cheese completely.

Cook the patties on a hot, lightly oiled grill or flat plate for 4–5 minutes each side, turning once. Serve on rolls with salad leaves and red pepper salsa.

Serves 6

Note: As a variation, try using Camembert, Brie, or any blue cheese instead of cheddar.

# Herb burgers

1 lb. 10 oz. ground lamb
2 tablespoons chopped basil
1 tablespoon chopped chives
1 tablespoon chopped rosemary
1 tablespoon chopped thyme
2 tablespoons lemon juice
1 cup fresh bread crumbs
1 egg
2 long crusty rolls
lettuce leaves, rinsed and dried
2 tomatoes, sliced
tomato sauce, to serve

Combine the lamb with the herbs, juice, bread crumbs, and egg and season well with salt and pepper. Mix well with your hands. Divide the mixture into eight portions and shape into thick, rectangular patties.

Place the burgers on a hot, lightly oiled grill or flat plate. Cook for 5–10 minutes each side or until well browned and just cooked through.

Cut the rolls in half and garnish with the burgers, lettuce, tomatoes, and tomato sauce.

Makes 8 burgers

## Brunch burgers with the works

1 lb. 10 oz. ground beef
1 onion, finely chopped
1 egg
1/2 cup fresh bread crumbs
2 tablespoons tomato paste
1 tablespoon Worcestershire sauce
2 tablespoons chopped Italian parsley
3 large onions
2 tablespoons butter
6 slices cheddar cheese
butter, extra, for cooking
6 eggs, extra
6 slices bacon
6 large hamburger buns, lightly
  toasted
shredded lettuce
2 tomatoes, thinly sliced
6 large beet slices, drained
6 pineapple rings, drained
tomato sauce, to serve

Mix together the beef, onion, egg, bread crumbs, tomato paste, Worcestershire sauce, and parsley with your hands. Season well. Divide into six portions and shape into patties. Cover and set aside.

Slice the onions into thin rings. Heat the butter on a barbecue flat plate. Cook the onion, turning often, until well browned. Move the onion to the outer edge of the flat plate to keep warm. Brush the grill or flat plate liberally with oil.

Cook the burgers for 3–4 minutes each side or until browned and cooked through. Move to the cooler part of the grill or transfer to a plate and keep warm. Place a slice of cheese on each burger.

Heat a small amount of butter on a barbecue flat plate or in a large frying pan. Fry the eggs and bacon until the eggs are cooked through and the bacon is golden and crisp. Fill the buns with lettuce, tomato, beets, and pineapple and top with a burger. Pile the onion, egg, bacon, and tomato sauce on top of the burger.

Serves 6

# Entrées

# Swordfish with tomato butter and grilled asparagus

7 tablespoons butter, softened
1/3 cup sun-dried tomatoes, finely chopped
2 tablespoons baby capers in brine, drained and crushed
1 1/2 tablespoons shredded basil leaves
4 garlic cloves, crushed
1/4 cup extra-virgin olive oil
10 1/2 oz. slender asparagus spears, trimmed
4 swordfish steaks

Put the butter in a bowl with the tomato, capers, basil, and two cloves of crushed garlic and mash it all together. Shape the flavored butter into a log, then wrap it in waxed paper and twist the ends to close them off. Refrigerate until the butter is firm, then cut it into 1/2-inch slices and leave it at room temperature, covered, until needed.

Mix 2 tablespoons of the oil and the remaining garlic in a small bowl. Toss the asparagus spears with the oil until they are well coated, season them with salt and pepper, and leave for 30 minutes.

Preheat a ridged barbecue grill to high heat. Brush the swordfish steaks with the remaining oil and cook them for 2–3 minutes on each side or until they are just cooked through. Don't overcook the fish, as residual heat will continue to cook the meat after it has been removed from the grill. Put a piece of the tomato butter on top of each steak as soon as it comes off the grill, then season to taste. Cook the asparagus on the flat plate, turning it regularly, for 2–3 minutes or until it is just tender. Serve the asparagus immediately with the fish.

Serves 4

## Sage and ricotta stuffed chicken

1 cup fresh ricotta cheese, well drained
1 tablespoon shredded sage leaves
2 garlic cloves, crushed
1½ teaspoons grated lemon zest
2 tablespoons finely grated Parmesan cheese
4 chicken breast fillets
8 thin slices prosciutto
olive oil, for brushing

Mix together the ricotta, sage, garlic, zest, and Parmesan until they are well combined. Use a sharp knife to cut a large pocket into the side of each chicken breast and fill each pocket with a quarter of the ricotta mixture. Pin the pockets closed with toothpicks and wrap each breast in two slices of prosciutto, securing it with a toothpick.

Heat a barbecue flat plate to medium, brush the chicken pockets with olive oil, and season them with freshly ground black pepper. Cook them for 8 minutes on each side or until they are cooked through. This is delicious served with baby spinach salad (see page 338).

Serves 4

# Greek pepper lamb salad

10½ oz. lamb sirloin
1½ tablespoons cracked black
  pepper
3 vine-ripened tomatoes, cut into
  8 wedges
2 cucumbers, sliced
5½ oz. kalamata olives, marinated in
  lemon and garlic, then drained
  (reserving 1½ tablespoons oil)
3½ oz. feta cheese, cubed
¾ teaspoon dried oregano
1 tablespoon lemon juice
1 tablespoon extra-virgin olive oil

Roll the lamb sirloin in the pepper, pressing the pepper on with your fingers. Cover and refrigerate for about 15 minutes. Place the tomato, cucumber, olives, feta, and ½ teaspoon of the dried oregano in a bowl.

Heat a grill pan or barbecue grill, brush with oil, and, when very hot, cook the lamb for 2–3 minutes on each side or until cooked to your liking. Keep warm.

Whisk the lemon juice, extra-virgin olive oil, reserved kalamata oil, and the remaining dried oregano together well. Season. Pour half the dressing over the salad, toss together, and arrange on a serving platter.

Cut the lamb diagonally into ½-inch-thick slices and arrange on top of the salad. Pour the rest of the dressing on top and serve.

Serves 4

## Moroccan squash on pistachio couscous

2 lb. 4 oz. squash
2 tablespoons olive oil
1 cup vegetable stock
1 cup instant couscous
1 cup plain yogurt
1 tablespoon lemon juice
1 tablespoon honey
1 tablespoon butter
2 garlic cloves, crushed
1 small onion, finely diced
2 tablespoons finely chopped Italian
  parsley
2 tablespoons finely chopped cilantro
¼ cup roasted, shelled, and roughly
  chopped pistachio nuts
2 tablespoons ras el hanout or
  Moroccan spice blend (see Note)

Peel the squash, cut it into ¾-inch-thick pieces, and toss it in a bowl with the olive oil and remaining spice mix. Preheat a covered barbecue to medium. Grill the squash, covered, for 45 minutes or until it is golden all over and cooked through.

Bring the vegetable stock to a boil, pour it over the couscous, and stir to combine them. Cover the bowl with plastic wrap and leave it for 10 minutes or until all of the stock has been absorbed.

Spoon the yogurt into a small bowl, stir in the lemon juice and honey, and season to taste.

Melt the butter in a small frying pan, add the garlic and onion, and cook them over low heat for 5 minutes or until they are softened. Add the onion mixture to the couscous with the parsley, cilantro, pistachio nuts, and 2 teaspoons of the spice mix, stir it together, and season to taste.

Pile the couscous onto a serving plate, top it with the grilled squash pieces, and serve with the yogurt dressing.

Serves 4–6

Note: Ras el hanout is a traditional Moroccan spice mix, and is available from gourmet food stores. The taste of this dish will rely on the quality of the spices used, so if you have time, make your own. Dry-fry 6 cardamom pods, ½ teaspoon black pepper, and 1 teaspoon fennel seeds until they are fragrant. Let the spices cool, then grind them in a spice grinder or mortar and pestle and mix with ½ teaspoon ground cinnamon, 1 teaspoon turmeric, ½ teaspoon cayenne pepper, 2 teaspoons mild paprika, 1 teaspoon ground cumin, ½ teaspoon allspice, and 1 teaspoon salt. The spice mix can be stored in an airtight container for up to 2 months.

## Chicken salad with arugula and cannellini beans

1/3 cup lemon juice
3 garlic cloves, crushed
1 teaspoon brown sugar
1/4 cup finely chopped basil
1/2 cup olive oil
4 chicken breast fillets
14-oz. can cannellini beans, rinsed
   and drained
3 1/2 oz. arugula leaves

Whisk together the lemon juice, garlic, sugar, basil, and olive oil and season lightly with salt and pepper. Pour a third of the dressing over the chicken to coat. Cook the chicken on a hot, lightly oiled barbecue grill or flat plate for 4 minutes on each side or until cooked through.

Meanwhile, combine the beans and arugula with the remaining dressing, toss well, and season. Slice the chicken and serve over the arugula and beans.

Serves 4

## Chipolatas with cheese and jalapeño quesadillas

2 tablespoons olive oil
2 garlic cloves, crushed
2 (14-oz.) cans crushed tomatoes
1/2 teaspoon ground cumin
16 (6-inch) flour tortillas
3 cups shredded cheddar cheese
1/3 cup pickled jalapeño chilies,
   drained and roughly chopped
20 spicy chipolatas
cilantro, to garnish

Heat the olive oil in a frying pan over medium heat and cook the garlic for 1–2 minutes or until it is just beginning to turn golden. Add the crushed tomatoes and cumin and season well. Reduce the heat to low and cook the relish for 30–35 minutes or until it becomes thick and pulpy.

In the meantime, sprinkle a tortilla with 1/3 cup of the grated cheese, leaving a 1/2-inch border around the edge. Sprinkle 1 1/2 teaspoons of the jalapeño chilies over the cheese and put another tortilla on top, pressing it down. Repeat the process with the remaining tortillas, cheese, and jalapeños to make eight quesadillas.

Preheat the barbecue to low heat. Cook the chipolatas on the flat plate, turning occasionally, for 10–12 minutes or until they are cooked through. When the chipolatas are nearly ready, start cooking the quesadillas on the grill for 1–2 minutes on each side or until the cheese has melted. You may need to do this in batches, so make sure you keep them warm as you go. Cut each quesadilla into quarters and serve with the tomato relish and chipolatas. Garnish with the cilantro.

Serves 4

# Vietnamese fish

1 lb. 10 oz. small, firm white fish
2 teaspoons green peppercorns,
  finely crushed
2 teaspoons chopped red chili
3 teaspoons fish sauce
2 teaspoons vegetable oil
1 tablespoon vegetable oil, extra
2 onions, finely sliced
1 1/2-inch piece fresh ginger, peeled
  and thinly sliced
3 garlic cloves, finely sliced
2 teaspoons sugar
4 scallions, cut into short lengths,
  then finely shredded

*Lemon and garlic dipping sauce*
3 tablespoons lemon juice
2 tablespoons fish sauce
1 tablespoon sugar
2 small red chilies, chopped
3 garlic cloves, crushed

Cut two diagonal slashes in the thickest part of the fish on both sides. In a food processor or mortar and pestle, grind the peppercorns, chili, and fish sauce to a paste and brush over the fish. Leave for 20 minutes.

To make the dipping sauce, mix together all the ingredients.

Cook the fish on a hot, lightly oiled grill or flat plate for 8 minutes on each side or until the flesh flakes easily when tested.

While the fish is cooking, heat the extra oil in a pan and stir the onion over medium heat until golden. Add the ginger, garlic, and sugar and cook for 3 minutes. Place the fish on a serving plate, top with the onion mixture, and sprinkle with scallions. Serve with the dipping sauce.

Serves 6

## Cilantro shrimp

8 raw jumbo shrimp
1 tablespoon sweet chili sauce
1 teaspoon ground coriander
$\frac{1}{2}$ cup olive oil
$\frac{1}{3}$ cup lime juice
3 garlic cloves, crushed
1 tomato, peeled, seeded, and
  chopped
2 tablespoons roughly chopped
  cilantro

Remove the heads from the shrimp
and cut the shrimp in half lengthwise
with a sharp knife, leaving the tails
attached. Pull out each dark vein.

Mix together the sweet chili sauce
and ground coriander with half the
olive oil, half the lime juice, and half
the garlic. Add the shrimp and toss
to coat, then cover and marinate in
the refrigerator for 30 minutes.

Meanwhile, to make the dressing, mix
the remaining olive oil, lime juice, and
garlic in a bowl with the chopped
tomato and cilantro.

Drain the shrimp, reserving the
marinade, and cook, cut-side down,
on a hot, lightly oiled grill or flat
plate for 1–2 minutes each side or
until cooked through, brushing
occasionally with the marinade.
Spoon a little of the dressing over
the shrimp and season well with
salt and pepper before serving.

Serves 4

## Marinated lamb cutlets with orange sweet potatoes and ginger nori butter

16 lamb cutlets
½ cup Japanese plum wine
  (see Note)
2 tablespoons soy sauce
1 teaspoon finely grated fresh ginger
2 garlic cloves, crushed
a few drops of sesame oil
4 orange sweet potatoes, 7 oz. each
vegetable oil, for brushing

*Ginger nori butter*
6 tablespoons butter, softened
1½ tablespoons very finely
  shredded nori
2 teaspoons finely grated fresh
  ginger

Trim the lamb cutlets of any excess fat. Mix together the plum wine, soy sauce, grated ginger, garlic, and sesame oil, add the cutlets to the marinade, and turn them a few times so they are well coated. Cover the dish with plastic wrap and refrigerate it for 3 hours.

To make the ginger nori butter, mash the butter, shredded nori, and grated ginger together and season to taste with pepper.

Preheat a covered barbecue to medium heat. Brush the sweet potatoes with a little oil and wrap in a double layer of foil. Put them on the grill and replace the lid. Roast the potatoes for 50 minutes or until they are tender when pierced with a sharp knife, then remove them from the heat and leave the barbecue uncovered.

Drain the marinade into a small saucepan and cook over high heat for 5 minutes or until it is reduced by about half. Brush the grill with a little oil and cook the cutlets for 1 minute, then turn them over, brush with the reduced marinade, and cook them for another minute. This will give a rare cutlet, so if you like your meat cooked a little more, you'll need to extend the cooking time on each side by a

minute or so. Remove the cutlets from the barbecue, brush them with the remaining reduced marinade, cover, and leave them to cool for 3 minutes. Serve the lamb with the orange sweet potatoes topped with nori butter. They are delicious with an Asian leaf salad (try a few handfuls each of mizuna, baby tatsoi, and Chinese cabbage) or lightly steamed Asian greens.

Serves 4

Note: Japanese plum wine is available at Asian markets.

# Chicken tikka with garlic naan and apple raita

⅓ cup tikka paste
¼ cup thick yogurt
1 lb. 5 oz. chicken breast fillets, cut
  into 1¼-inch cubes
2 small red onions, quartered
vegetable oil, for brushing
2 tablespoons chopped cilantro

*Apple raita*
1 green apple, grated
2 teaspoons lemon juice
¼ cup sour cream
3 tablespoons chopped mint leaves

*Garlic naan*
1 garlic clove, crushed
2 tablespoons butter, softened
4 plain naan breads

Stir the tikka paste and yogurt together, add the chicken, and turn it until it is evenly coated in the tikka mixture. Cover the chicken with plastic wrap and refrigerate it for 4 hours or overnight.

To make the raita, put the grated apple, lemon juice, sour cream, and mint in a small bowl and stir it all together. Cover the bowl and refrigerate it until ready to serve. Mash the crushed garlic and butter together and brush one side of each piece of naan with about 2 teaspoons of garlic butter.

Soak four wooden skewers in cold water for 1 hour and preheat the barbecue to low–medium heat. Thread the chicken and onion pieces onto the skewers and cook them on the flat plate for 5–6 minutes on each side, turning once. A few minutes before the chicken is ready, lightly brush the grill with some oil. Grill the naan, buttered-side down, for 1–2 minutes or until the bread is golden and marked. Turn it and grill for another minute on the other side.

Sprinkle the skewers with the chopped cilantro and serve them with the garlic naan and apple raita.

Serves 4

## Pepper steaks with horseradish sauce

4 sirloin steaks
3 tablespoons seasoned cracked
    black pepper

*Horseradish sauce*
2 tablespoons brandy
3 tablespoons beef stock
4 tablespoons cream
1 tablespoon horseradish cream
$1/2$ teaspoon sugar

Coat the steaks on both sides with pepper, pressing it into the meat. Cook on a hot, lightly oiled barbecue grill or flat plate for 5–10 minutes or until cooked to your taste.

To make the sauce, put the brandy and stock in a pan. Bring to a boil, then reduce the heat. Stir in the cream, horseradish, and sugar and heat through. Serve with the steaks.

Serves 4

## Thai red chicken with jasmine rice and Asian greens

1 tablespoon red curry paste
1 cup coconut cream
3 kaffir lime leaves
4 chicken breast fillets, tenderloin
  removed
2 cups jasmine rice
1 cup chicken stock
1 tablespoon soy sauce
1 garlic clove, bruised
$3/4$ x $3/4$-inch piece fresh ginger,
  bruised
1 lb. 10 oz. Chinese broccoli, washed
  and tied in a bunch
cilantro sprigs, to garnish

Mix together the curry paste, coconut cream, and kaffir lime leaves, then add the chicken and turn it so that it is coated in the marinade. Cover the bowl and refrigerate it for at least 4 hours or overnight.

Half an hour before you are ready to cook the chicken, wash the rice in a sieve until the water runs clear. Put the rice in a saucepan with 3 cups water and bring it to a boil for 1 minute. Cover the saucepan with a tightly fitting lid, reduce the heat to as low as possible, and let it cook for 10 minutes. Without removing the lid, remove the pan from the heat and leave it for at least 10 minutes or until you are ready to eat. Meanwhile, bring the chicken stock, soy sauce, garlic, and ginger to a boil in a small saucepan for 5 minutes or until it is reduced by half. Strain the mixture, return the liquid to the saucepan, and keep it warm.

Bring a large pot of salted water to a boil and add the Chinese broccoli, stalk-side down. Cook for 2–3 minutes or until it is just tender, then drain well and arrange it on a serving dish. Just before serving, pour the hot chicken stock mixture over the greens.

Preheat the flat grill plate to medium. Cook the chicken for 7–8 minutes on each side or until it is cooked through. Transfer the chicken to a plate, cover it loosely with foil, and leave it to cool. Fluff the rice with a fork and put it in a serving bowl. Garnish the chicken with the cilantro and serve it with the rice and Chinese broccoli.

Serves 4

## Sumac-crusted lamb fillets with baba ghanoush

2 tablespoons olive oil
1 lb. 10 oz. small new potatoes
2–3 garlic cloves, crushed
1/4 cup lemon juice
1 red pepper, seeded and quartered
    lengthwise
4 lamb sirloins, about 7 oz. each
1 tablespoon sumac (if unavailable,
    use ground cumin)
3 tablespoons finely chopped Italian
    parsley
1 cup good-quality baba ghanoush
    (eggplant dip)

Heat the oil in a saucepan big enough to hold the potatoes in one layer. Add the potatoes and garlic and cook, turning frequently, for 3–5 minutes. When golden, add the lemon juice and reduce the heat to medium–low. Simmer, covered, for 15–20 minutes or until tender, stirring occasionally to prevent sticking. Remove from the heat and season well.

Meanwhile, lightly oil a grill and heat to very hot. Cook the pepper, skin-side down, for 1–2 minutes or until the skin starts to blister and turn black. Cook the other side for 1–2 minutes. Place in a plastic bag and set aside.

Coat the lamb with sumac. Cook on the grill for 4–5 minutes on each side or until cooked to your liking. Remove from the heat, cover with foil, and let cool. Remove the skin from the pepper and slice the quarters into thin strips.

Stir the parsley through the potatoes. Divide the baba ghanoush among four plates. Cut the lamb into 1/2-inch slices diagonally and arrange on top of the baba ghanoush with the pepper strips. Serve with the potatoes and a green salad.

Serves 4

## Veal steaks with caper butter

4 tablespoons butter, softened
2 tablespoons dry white wine
2 tablespoons capers, finely chopped
2 teaspoons finely grated lemon zest
8 small veal steaks, about 1 lb. 2 oz.
  in total
mixed salad greens, to serve

Mix together the butter, white wine, capers, lemon zest, and some salt and black pepper with a wooden spoon. Shape into a log, cover, and refrigerate until needed.

Cook the veal steaks on a hot, lightly oiled barbecue flat plate or grill for 2–3 minutes on each side. Remove, place on warm plates, and top with slices of the caper butter. Serve immediately on a bed of salad greens.

Serves 4

# Portuguese spatchcock

1 red onion, chopped
6 garlic cloves, chopped
3 teaspoons grated lemon zest
2 teaspoons chili flakes
1 1/2 teaspoons paprika
1/4 cup vegetable oil
1/4 cup red wine vinegar
4 spatchcocks (split chickens),
  1 lb. 2 oz. each
1/3 cup chopped Italian parsley
lemon halves

Put the onion, garlic, lemon zest, chili flakes, paprika, oil, and vinegar in a food processor and blend them to a smooth paste.

Cut each of the spatchcocks down the backbone with sharp kitchen scissors and press down on the breastbone to flatten it out. Score the flesh and brush it with the spice mixture, then put the spatchcocks in a nonmetallic dish, cover, and refrigerate overnight.

Preheat the grill to low–medium heat. Grill the spatchcocks for 10 minutes on each side or until they are cooked through (test by piercing the thigh with a skewer—if the juices run clear, they are ready), then sprinkle with parsley and serve with the lemon halves.

Serves 4

Note: Try grilling the lemon halves for a bit of extra flavor.

## Piri piri shrimp

2 lb. 4 oz. large raw shrimp
4 long red chilies, seeded
$3/4$ cup white wine vinegar
2 large garlic cloves, chopped
6–8 small red chilies, chopped
$1/2$ cup olive oil
$5 1/2$ oz. mixed lettuce leaves

Remove the heads from the shrimp and slice them down the back without cutting right through, leaving the tail intact. Open out each shrimp and remove the dark vein, then store the prepared shrimp in the refrigerator while you make the sauce.

To make the sauce, put the long chilies in a saucepan with the vinegar and simmer them over medium–high heat for 5 minutes or until the chilies are soft. Let the mixture cool slightly, then put the chilies and 1/4 cup of the vinegar in a food processor. Add the garlic and chopped small chilies and blend until the mixture is smooth. While the motor is running, gradually add the oil and remaining vinegar to the food processor.

Put the shrimp in the marinade, making sure they are well coated, then cover them and refrigerate for 30 minutes.

Take the shrimp out of the marinade, bring the marinade to a boil, and let it simmer for 5 minutes or until it is slightly thickened and reduced. Take the shrimp and the marinade out to the barbecue and leave the saucepan with the marinade in it on the edge of the barbecue to keep it warm.

Lightly oil the grill and heat it to high. Cook the shrimp, basting them with the marinade, for 2–3 minutes on each side or until they are cooked through. Arrange the lettuce on four plates, top it with the shrimp, and serve immediately with the chili sauce.

Serves 4

# Grilled vegetables with basil aioli

*Basil aioli*
1 garlic clove
1/4 cup torn basil leaves
1 egg yolk
1/2 cup olive oil
2 teaspoons lemon juice

2 large red peppers, quartered, core and seeds removed
1 eggplant, cut into 1/4-inch-thick rounds
1 orange sweet potato, peeled and cut diagonally into 1/4-inch-thick rounds
3 zucchini, sliced lengthwise into 1/4-inch-thick slices
2 red onions, cut into 1/2-inch-thick rounds
1/3 cup olive oil
1 loaf Turkish bread, split and cut into 4 equal pieces

To make the basil aioli, put the garlic, basil, and egg yolk in a food processor and blend until smooth. With the motor running, gradually add the oil in a thin stream until the mixture thickens. Stir in the lemon juice and season to taste. Cover and refrigerate until ready to serve.

Preheat a barbecue grill to medium. Put the pepper, skin-side down, around the cool edge of the grill and cook it for 8–10 minutes or until the skin has softened and is blistering.

Meanwhile, brush the eggplant, sweet potato, zucchini, and onion slices on both sides with olive oil and season them lightly. Cook the vegetables in batches on the middle of the grill for 5–8 minutes or until they are cooked through but still firm. As the vegetable pieces cook, put them on a tray in a single layer to prevent them from steaming, then grill the Turkish bread on both sides until it is lightly marked and toasted.

Spread both cut sides of the bread with 1 tablespoon of basil aioli and pile some of the grilled vegetables on top. Top with the remaining toast and serve immediately.

Serves 4

# Beef fajitas

1 lb. 12 oz. rump steak
2 teaspoons ground cumin
1 teaspoon ground oregano
1 teaspoon paprika
2 tablespoons Worcestershire sauce
1 tablespoon soy sauce
3 garlic cloves
1/4 cup lime juice
1 large onion, thinly sliced
1 red pepper, cut into 1/4-inch strips
1 green pepper, cut into 1/4-inch strips
1 tablespoon olive oil
8 flour tortillas
1 ripe avocado, diced
2 ripe Roma tomatoes, diced
1/2 cup grated cheddar cheese
1/3 cup sour cream

Trim the steak of any fat and give it a good pounding with a meat mallet on both sides. Mix the cumin, oregano, paprika, Worcestershire sauce, soy sauce, garlic, and lime juice in a shallow nonmetallic dish and add the beef. Turn until well coated in the marinade, then cover and refrigerate for at least 4 hours or overnight.

Drain the steak, reserving the marinade, and pat it dry with paper towels. Simmer the marinade in a small saucepan over medium heat for 5 minutes or until it is reduced by about half, and keep it warm.

Preheat a barbecue to high. Toss the onion and pepper with the oil, then spread them across the flat plate, turning every so often, for 10 minutes or until cooked through and caramelized. While the vegetables are cooking, cook the steak on the grill for 3 minutes each side or until cooked to your liking. Remove it from the heat and let it cool, covered, for 5 minutes. Thinly slice the steak and arrange it on a plate with the onion and pepper strips and serve with the tortillas, avocado, tomato, cheese, sour cream, and marinade sauce. Let everyone fill their own tortillas.

Serves 4–6

## Crispy chicken wings

12 chicken wings
3 tablespoons soy sauce
3 tablespoons hoisin sauce
1/2 cup tomato sauce
2 tablespoons honey
1 tablespoon brown sugar
1 tablespoon cider vinegar
2 garlic cloves, crushed
1/4 teaspoon Chinese five-spice
  powder
2 teaspoons sesame oil

Tuck the chicken wing tips to the underside and place in a nonmetallic bowl. Mix together all the remaining ingredients and pour over the wings, tossing to coat. Cover and leave in the refrigerator for at least 2 hours, turning occasionally. Drain, reserving the marinade.

Cook the wings on a hot, lightly oiled barbecue grill or flat plate for 5 minutes or until cooked through, brushing with the reserved marinade several times.

Serves 6

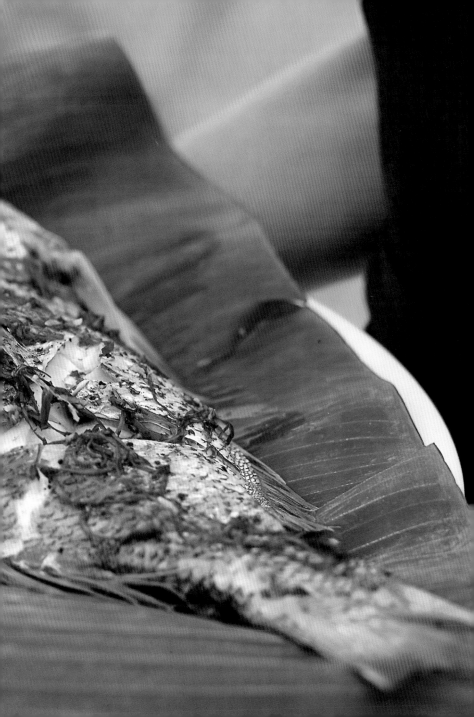

# Snapper envelope with ginger and scallions

*Dressing*
1 scallion
3 tablespoons chopped cilantro
  leaves
1 teaspoon finely grated fresh
  ginger
2 tablespoons lime juice
1 tablespoon fish sauce
½ teaspoon sesame oil

1 whole snapper, about 4 lb. 4 oz.
sea salt
1 lime
4 scallions
1 cup cilantro
1 tablespoon finely grated fresh
  ginger
vegetable oil spray

To make the dressing, finely slice the green part of the scallion and mix together with the cilantro, ginger, lime juice, fish sauce, and sesame oil.

Check that the snapper has been thoroughly scaled, then wash it under cold running water and pat it dry with paper towels. In the thickest part of the flesh, make diagonal cuts $1/2$ inch apart in one direction and then in the other direction, so that the flesh is scored in a diamond pattern. Lightly season the fish with sea salt and freshly ground black pepper.

Peel the lime, removing all the pith, with a small, sharp knife and separate the lime sections by carefully cutting each piece away from the membrane. Slice the scallions diagonally, mix them with the cilantro, lime segments, and ginger, and stuff the mixture into the cavity of the fish.

Lightly spray a double layer of foil with vegetable oil, making sure it is large enough to wrap around the fish and totally enclose it. Fold the foil around the fish and seal the edges tightly.

Preheat a covered barbecue to medium indirect heat. Put the fish in the middle of the barbecue and cook it, covered, for 10 minutes. Use a large metal spatula to turn the fish so that it will brown evenly on both sides and cook it for another 8–10 minutes or until it flakes when tested in the thickest part of the flesh.

When the fish is cooked, open the foil envelope and slide it onto a serving plate. Pour the cooking juices over the fish, drizzle the dressing over the top, and serve immediately. It is delicious with steamed jasmine rice and a green salad.

Serves 4

# Ginger-orange pork

6 pork butterfly steaks
1 cup ginger wine
½ cup orange marmalade
2 tablespoons vegetable oil
1 tablespoon grated fresh ginger

Trim the pork steak of excess fat and sinew. Mix together the wine, marmalade, oil, and ginger. Place the steaks in a shallow nonmetallic dish and add the marinade. Store, covered with plastic wrap, in the refrigerator for at least 3 hours, turning occasionally. Drain, reserving the marinade.

Cook the pork on a hot, lightly oiled barbecue flat plate or grill for 5 minutes each side or until tender, turning once.

While the meat is cooking, place the reserved marinade in a small pan. Bring to a boil, reduce the heat, and simmer for 5 minutes or until the marinade has reduced and thickened slightly. Pour over the pork.

Serves 6

Hint: Steaks of uneven thickness may curl when cooked. Prevent this by leaving a layer of fat on the outside and making a few deep cuts in it prior to cooking. Remove before serving.

# Lamb cutlets with mint gremolata

4 tablespoons mint leaves
1 tablespoon Italian parsley
2 garlic cloves
1½ tablespoons lemon zest (white pith removed), cut into thin strips
2 tablespoons extra-virgin olive oil
8 French-trimmed lamb cutlets
2 carrots
2 zucchini
1 tablespoon lemon juice

To make the gremolata, finely chop the mint, parsley, garlic, and lemon strips, then combine well.

Heat a barbecue grill or flat plate until very hot. Lightly brush with 1 tablespoon of the oil. Season the cutlets and cook over medium heat for 2 minutes on each side or until cooked to your liking. Remove the cutlets and cover to keep warm.

Trim the ends from the carrots and zucchini and, using a vegetable peeler, peel the vegetables lengthwise into ribbons. Heat the remaining oil in a large saucepan, add the vegetables, and toss over medium heat for 3–5 minutes or until sautéed but tender. Season lightly.

Divide the lamb cutlets among the serving plates, sprinkle the cutlets with the gremolata, and drizzle with the lemon juice. Serve with the vegetable ribbons.

Serves 4

## Bruschetta with mushrooms and mustard crème fraîche

5 small field mushrooms (about
   10$\frac{1}{2}$ oz.), quartered
1 red onion, halved and thinly sliced
$\frac{2}{3}$ cup olive oil
3 garlic cloves, crushed
1 $\frac{1}{2}$ tablespoons chopped oregano
   leaves
$\frac{1}{4}$ cup crème fraîche
1 teaspoon Dijon mustard
1 loaf ciabatta bread
$\frac{1}{4}$ cup olive oil, extra
1 large garlic clove, extra, peeled
   and halved
small oregano leaves, for garnish
6 handfuls mixed lettuce leaves
2 tablespoons extra-virgin olive oil
1 tablespoon lemon juice

Put the mushrooms and onion in separate bowls and season each well. Whisk together the oil, garlic, and oregano and pour two-thirds of the mixture over the mushrooms and the rest over the onion. Toss until well coated in the marinade, then cover and refrigerate for 30 minutes. Mix the crème fraîche and mustard together, then refrigerate it until needed.

Heat a barbecue to medium heat. Cut the bread into twelve $\frac{1}{2}$-inch-thick slices and brush both sides of each slice with the extra oil. Toast the bread on the grill for 1–2 minutes on each side or until golden and lightly charred, then rub one side of each slice with the cut side of the garlic clove. Cook the onion on the flat plate, tossing gently, for 2–3 minutes or until soft and golden. Cook the mushrooms on the flat plate for 2 minutes each side or until cooked through, then toss the onion and mushrooms together.

Arrange the mushrooms and onion on the garlic side of the bread slices and top with a teaspoon of mustard crème fraîche. Garnish with oregano leaves and season. Toss the lettuce leaves with the extra-virgin olive oil and lemon juice and serve with the bruschetta.

Serves 6

# Miso-glazed salmon and eggplant salad with sesame dressing

5 tablespoons sesame seeds, lightly toasted
1/4 cup white miso
1 tablespoon sake
1 tablespoon mirin
1 tablespoon sugar
1/4 cup dashi stock
1 large eggplant, cut into 1/2-inch rounds
2 garlic cloves, crushed
1/4 cup olive oil
2 teaspoons dark soy sauce
1/4 cup dashi stock, extra
1 teaspoon sugar, extra
1 teaspoon grated fresh ginger
5 1/2 oz. snow pea shoots
14 oz. daikon radishes, julienned
4 salmon fillets, skin removed

To make the miso glaze, put the sesame seeds in a spice grinder or mortar and pestle and grind until they have a rough, flaky texture. Whisk the miso, sake, mirin, sugar, and dashi stock together until smooth and stir in half of the crushed sesame seeds.

Put the eggplant rounds in a large bowl with the combined garlic and oil, season them well, and toss until the rounds are well coated.

To make the dressing, whisk together the soy sauce, extra dashi and sugar, ginger, and the remaining crushed sesame seeds. Put the snow pea shoots and daikon in a large bowl, add the soy dressing, and toss until well combined. Cover and refrigerate until needed.

Heat a barbecue to medium–high heat. Grill the eggplant for 3–4 minutes on each side or until it has softened, then allow it to cool slightly and cut it into quarters. Brush both sides of each salmon fillet with the miso glaze and cook them on the flat plate for 2 minutes each side or until they are almost cooked through, brushing with the glaze while they are cooking. Flake the fillets with a fork and toss them through the salad with the eggplant. Season and serve.

Serves 4

## Lemon and thyme roasted chicken with zucchini

1 (4-lb.) whole chicken
12 garlic cloves, unpeeled
10 sprigs lemon thyme
1 lemon, halved
1 tablespoon olive oil
8 small zucchini, halved lengthwise
2 tablespoons chopped Italian parsley
1 tablespoon all-purpose flour
1 cup chicken stock

Remove the giblets and any large fat deposits from inside the chicken, then pat it dry inside and out with paper towels. Season the cavity with salt and pepper and stuff it with the unpeeled garlic cloves and the sprigs of thyme. Rub the skin with the cut lemon, making sure that it is evenly coated all over, then brush it with 2 teaspoons of the oil and season with salt and black pepper. Tie the legs together.

Preheat a covered barbecue to medium indirect heat, with a drip tray underneath the grill. Position the chicken on the barbecue directly over the drip tray, close the hood, and roast the chicken for 1 hour or until the juices run clear when it is pierced with a skewer between the thigh and the body.

When the chicken has been cooking for about 40 minutes, toss the zucchini with the remaining olive oil and season it with salt and black pepper. Arrange the zucchini on the grill around the chicken, re-cover the grill, and cook the chicken and the zucchini for 20–25 minutes or until the zucchini is tender but not soggy. Put the zucchini in a serving dish and sprinkle it with the parsley. When the chicken is ready, remove it from the barbecue, cover it loosely with foil,

and leave it to cool for 10 minutes. Remove the garlic from the chicken cavity but do not peel the cloves.

If you would like gravy to go with the chicken, pour the contents of the drip tray into a container and skim off as much fat as possible. Tip the remaining juices into a saucepan, add the flour, and stir well to combine. Cook the gravy over medium heat for 3–4 minutes or until it has thickened, then add the chicken stock and any juices that have been released from the chicken while it was resting. Bring the gravy to a boil, then reduce the heat and simmer it for 3–4 minutes. Season the gravy to taste, strain it into a pitcher, and serve with the chicken, garlic, and zucchini.

Serves 4

## Thai beef salad

1/3 cup lime juice
2 tablespoons fish sauce
2 teaspoons brown sugar
1 garlic clove, crushed
1 tablespoon finely chopped cilantro
   roots and stems
1 stem lemongrass (white part only),
   finely chopped
2 small red chilies, finely sliced
2 beef eye fillet steaks, 7 oz. each
5 1/2 oz. mixed salad leaves
1/2 red onion, cut into thin wedges
1/2 cup cilantro
1/3 cup torn mint leaves
9 oz. cherry tomatoes, halved
1 small cucumber, halved lengthwise
   and thinly sliced diagonally

Mix together the lime juice, fish
sauce, brown sugar, garlic, chopped
cilantro, lemongrass, and chili until the
sugar has dissolved.

Preheat a grill to medium–high heat
and cook the steaks for 4 minutes on
each side or until medium. Let the
steaks cool, then slice thinly across
the grain.

Put the salad leaves, onion, cilantro,
mint, tomatoes, and cucumber in
a large bowl, add the beef and
dressing, toss them together, and
serve immediately.

Serves 4

## Barbecued chermoula shrimp

2 lb. 4 oz. raw medium shrimp
3 teaspoons hot paprika
2 teaspoons ground cumin
1 cup Italian parsley
1/2 cup cilantro
1/4 cup lemon juice
1/2 cup olive oil
1 1/2 cups couscous
1 tablespoon grated lemon zest
lemon wedges, to serve

Peel the shrimp, leaving the tails intact, and discard the heads. Gently pull out the dark vein from the backs, starting at the head end. Place the shrimp in a large bowl. Dry-fry the paprika and cumin in a frying pan for about 1 minute or until fragrant. Remove from the heat.

Blend or process the spices, parsley, cilantro, lemon juice, and 1/2 cup of the oil until finely chopped. Add a little salt and pepper. Pour over the shrimp and mix well, then cover with plastic wrap and refrigerate for 10 minutes. Heat a grill pan or barbecue grill until hot.

Meanwhile, to cook the couscous, bring 1 cup water to a boil in a saucepan and stir in the couscous, lemon zest, the remaining oil, and 1/4 teaspoon salt. Remove from the heat, cover, and leave for 5 minutes. Fluff the couscous with a fork, adding a little extra olive oil if needed.

Cook the shrimp on the grill for about 3–4 minutes or until cooked through, turning and brushing with extra marinade while cooking (be careful not to overcook). Serve the shrimp on a bed of couscous with a wedge of lemon.

Serves 4

## Hoisin lamb with charred scallions

1 lb. 12 oz. lamb loin
¼ cup hoisin sauce
2 tablespoons soy sauce
2 garlic cloves, bruised
1 tablespoon grated fresh ginger
2 teaspoons olive oil
16 scallions, trimmed to 7 inches long
¼ cup chopped toasted peanuts

Trim the lamb of any excess fat and sinew. Combine the hoisin sauce, soy sauce, garlic, ginger, and 1 teaspoon of the oil in a shallow dish, add the lamb, and turn it so that it is well coated in the marinade. Cover the dish and refrigerate for 4 hours or overnight.

Toss the trimmed scallions with the remaining oil and season them well. Remove the lamb from the marinade, season the meat, and pour the marinade into a small saucepan. Simmer the marinade for 5 minutes or until it is slightly reduced. Preheat a grill to medium heat. Cook the lamb for 5–6 minutes on each side or until it is cooked to your liking, brushing it frequently with the reduced marinade, then let it cool, covered, for 3 minutes. Grill the scallions for 1–2 minutes or until they are tender but still firm.

Cut the lamb across the grain into ³/₄-inch-thick slices and arrange it on a serving plate. Drizzle any juices that have been released during cooling over the lamb and sprinkle it with the toasted peanuts. Serve with the scallions. This is delicious with Asian rice salad (see page 317).

Serves 4

## Spiced duck breast with peach and chili salad

6 ripe peaches
1 lime plus 1 tablespoon lime juice, extra
1 tablespoon extra-virgin olive oil
1 small red chili, seeded and finely sliced
2 tablespoons chopped mint leaves
4 duck breasts
2 teaspoons ground coriander
lime wedges

Dip the peaches into a saucepan of boiling water for 5 seconds, then plunge into ice water. Remove the skins, which should slip off easily. Cut each peach in half, remove the pit, then cut each half into eight wedges. Peel the lime, removing all the pith, and separate the lime sections by carefully cutting each piece away from the membrane. Toss the peach slices with the lime segments, extra lime juice, olive oil, chili, and mint and season with a little pepper.

Trim the duck breasts of fat and sinew and sprinkle each breast with the ground coriander.

Preheat a barbecue flat plate to medium heat and cook the duck on the flat plate for 4 minutes or until the skin is golden, then turn it and cook for another 4 minutes. Turn the breasts over again and cook them for another minute to make the skin crispy, then leave to cool in a warm place for 10 minutes.

Slice each breast diagonally into four pieces and serve them with the peach salad and lime wedges.

Serves 4

# Bourbon-glazed beef ribs with sweet potatoes

*Marinade*
1/4 teaspoon chili powder
1/2 teaspoon chili flakes
1/2 teaspoon celery salt
1/8 teaspoon cayenne pepper
2 cups cider vinegar
1/4 cup lemon juice
6 garlic cloves, crushed
1 tablespoon paprika
1 teaspoon garlic powder
1 teaspoon onion powder
1/2 cup Worcestershire sauce

6 lb. 8 oz. beef shortribs

*Sweet potatoes*
5 tablespoons butter, at room
    temperature
1 tablespoon maple syrup
1 tablespoon chopped pecans
1/2 teaspoon garlic salt
4 sweet potatoes, 7 oz. each

*Barbecue sauce*
2 cups tomato sauce
1/4 cup brown sugar
1/3 cup bourbon
1/4 cup Dijon mustard
1 tablespoon hot pepper sauce
2 teaspoons paprika
1 teaspoon garlic powder
1 teaspoon onion powder
1 1/2 tablespoons Worcestershire sauce

Put the marinade ingredients in a bowl with 1/4 teaspoon pepper and 1/4 teaspoon salt, mix together well, and rub the marinade all over the ribs. Put the ribs in a nonmetallic bowl, cover, and refrigerate overnight.

Mash together the butter, maple syrup, pecans, garlic salt, and some black pepper and cover until ready to serve.

Put the barbecue sauce ingredients in a saucepan and stir together. Simmer over low heat for 15 minutes or until the mixture has thickened, stirring constantly. Be careful while stirring the sauce, as it might splatter a bit.

Preheat a covered barbecue to very low indirect heat. Remove the ribs from the marinade and baste them all over with the barbecue sauce. Cook them on the flat plate for 3 hours or until they are very tender, turning and basting them every 30 minutes.

Arrange the whole sweet potatoes on a lightly greased baking tray and add them to the barbecue 45 minutes before the ribs have finished cooking.

Remove the ribs and sweet potatoes from the barbecue, slice each sweet potato down the middle, and top each with some of the flavored butter.

Cut between the ribs to separate them and serve the ribs with the sweet potatoes.

Serves 4–6

Notes: Beef shortribs are also known as beef loin ribs.

Make sure the temperature of the barbecue remains low and constant. If the heat is too high, the ribs will burn before they become tender.

# Stuffed eggplant

2 eggplants
2 tablespoons olive oil
1 onion, chopped
2 garlic cloves, crushed
4 tomatoes, roughly chopped
2 teaspoons tomato paste
2 tablespoons chopped dill
2 tablespoons chopped Italian parsley
2 tablespoons currants
2 tablespoons pine nuts
1 tablespoon red wine vinegar
1½ cups finely grated kefalotiri
   cheese

Cut each eggplant in half lengthwise and use a sharp knife to cut out the flesh, leaving a ¼-inch-thick shell. Finely dice the flesh, toss it with 2 teaspoons of salt, and drain it in a colander over a bowl for 30 minutes. Squeeze out any excess moisture from the eggplant, rinse it under cold water, and drain well on paper towels.

Heat 1 tablespoon oil in a frying pan over high heat. Add the diced eggplant and cook it, stirring frequently, for 5 minutes or until browned. Transfer to a large bowl. Heat the remaining olive oil in the frying pan over medium heat, cook the onion and garlic for 2 minutes, then add the tomato, tomato paste, dill, parsley, currants, pine nuts, and vinegar. Stir it all together and cook for 8–10 minutes, stirring occasionally. Add the tomato mixture to the eggplant with 1 cup of the kefalotiri, season with black pepper, and mix it together well.

Spoon the vegetable mixture into the eggplant shells and sprinkle with the remaining cheese. Preheat a covered barbecue to medium indirect heat and put the eggplants in the middle of the barbecue. Cover and cook for 30 minutes or until cooked through. Serve with a green salad.

Serves 4

# Tuna steaks with salsa and garlic mashed potatoes

*Garlic mashed potatoes*
6 medium floury potatoes (such as russet), cut into chunks
6–8 garlic cloves, peeled
1/3 cup milk
1/4 cup olive oil

*Salsa*
1 tablespoon olive oil
2 French shallots, finely chopped
1 cup green olives, pitted and quartered lengthwise
1/4 cup currants, soaked in warm water for 10 minutes
1 tablespoon baby capers, rinsed and squeezed dry
1 tablespoon sherry vinegar
2 tablespoons shredded mint leaves

4 tuna steaks, about 5 1/2 oz. each
olive oil, for brushing
sea salt

Boil the potato chunks and garlic for 10–15 minutes or until tender. Drain, then return the pan to the heat, shaking it to evaporate any excess water. Remove the pan from the heat and mash the potatoes and garlic until smooth, then stir in the milk and olive oil and season with salt and freshly ground black pepper.

To make the salsa, heat the oil in a frying pan over medium heat. Cook the shallots for 2–4 minutes or until they are softened but not browned, then add the olives, drained currants, and capers. Cook for 2 minutes, stirring continuously, then add the vinegar and cook for 2 minutes or until the liquid is reduced by about half. Remove the pan from the heat and keep the salsa warm until ready to serve.

Preheat a barbecue grill to medium–high heat. Brush the tuna steaks with olive oil, season them well with sea salt and freshly ground black pepper, and grill for 2–3 minutes each side for medium-rare or until they are cooked to your liking. Stir the mint into the salsa and serve it immediately with the garlic mashed potatoes and tuna.

Serves 4

# Malaysian barbecued seafood

1 onion, grated
4 garlic cloves, chopped
2-inch piece of fresh ginger, grated
3 stems lemongrass (white part only), chopped
2 teaspoons ground or grated fresh turmeric
1 teaspoon shrimp paste
1/3 cup vegetable oil
1/4 teaspoon salt
4 medium calamari tubes
2 thick white boneless fish fillets
8 raw jumbo shrimp
banana leaves, for serving
2 limes, cut into wedges
strips of lime zest, to garnish
mint leaves, to garnish

Combine the onion, garlic, ginger, lemongrass, turmeric, shrimp paste, oil, and salt in a small food processor. Process in short bursts until the mixture forms a paste.

Cut the calamari in half lengthwise and lay them on a board with the soft insides facing up. Score a very fine honeycomb pattern into the soft sides, being careful not to cut all the way through, and then cut into large pieces. Wash all the seafood under cold running water and pat dry with paper towels. Brush lightly with the spice paste, then place on a tray, cover, and refrigerate for 15 minutes.

Lightly oil a grill and heat. When the plate is hot, arrange the fish fillets and shrimp on the plate. Cook, turning once only, for about 3 minutes each side or until the fish flesh is just firm and the shrimp turn from bright pink to orange. Add the calamari pieces and cook for about 2 minutes or until the flesh turns white and rolls up. Be careful not to overcook the seafood.

Arrange the seafood on a platter lined with the banana leaves, add the lime wedges, and serve immediately, garnished with strips of lime zest and some fresh mint.

Serves 4

## Crispy-skinned salmon salad niçoise

14 oz. (about 3 medium) fingerling
    potatoes, washed
1 tablespoon olive oil
sea salt
12 quail eggs
2 cups small green beans
2 teaspoons olive oil, extra
3 salmon fillets, 7 oz. each
2 large ripe tomatoes, cut into
    8 wedges
½ cup small black olives
⅓ cup extra-virgin olive oil
1½ tablespoons white wine vinegar
1 tablespoon lemon juice
2 garlic cloves, crushed

Boil or steam the potatoes for 10 minutes or until they are almost cooked through. Drain and cut them diagonally into 3/4-inch slices, then toss them with the olive oil until they are coated. Season to taste with sea salt.

Put the eggs in a saucepan of cold water and bring them to a boil for 2 minutes. Cool the eggs under running water, then peel and halve them. Bring the water back to a boil and cook the beans for 2 minutes or until they are just tender, then drain them, plunge them into cold water, and drain again.

Heat the barbecue to medium–high heat. Cook the potato slices on the grill for 2 minutes on each side or until they are golden and cooked through. Brush the salmon fillets with the extra oil and cook them, skin-side down, on the flat plate for 2–3 minutes, then turn and cook them for another 2–3 minutes or until they are almost cooked through. The salmon should remain slightly rare in the middle. Break the fillets into chunks with a fork, removing any bones as you go.

Put the potatoes in a large bowl with the beans, tomatoes, and olives. Whisk together the oil, vinegar, lemon juice, and garlic and add the dressing to the bowl. Season with sea salt and freshly ground black pepper and gently toss the salad until everything is well combined. Pile some of the potato mixture on four serving plates, top with the salmon and eggs, and serve immediately.

Serves 4

# Pork loin with apple glaze and potato wedges

1 teaspoon aniseed
½ cup applesauce
2 tablespoons brown sugar
3 lb. 5 oz. boned pork loin with the
  skin on
2 teaspoons vegetable oil
4 large potatoes, each cut into
  8 wedges
2 tablespoons olive oil
2 teaspoons garlic salt

Dry-fry the aniseed over medium heat for 30 seconds or until it becomes fragrant. Add the applesauce and brown sugar, reduce the heat to low, and cook, stirring, for 1 minute.

Use a sharp knife to remove the skin from the pork loin. Score the skin in a diamond pattern and rub the oil and 1 tablespoon salt over the skin, working into the cuts. Put the potato wedges in a bowl with the olive oil and garlic salt, season with black pepper, and toss until well coated.

Preheat a covered barbecue to medium indirect heat. Tie the pork loin with string to help keep its shape, then put the pork and the skin in the barbecue and arrange the wedges around them. After 30 minutes, baste the pork with the apple glaze and repeat every 10 minutes for another 30 minutes (for a total of 1 hour cooking time). Turn the skin and the wedges as you go so that they cook evenly.

When the pork is ready, remove it from the barbecue and leave to cool, covered, for 10 minutes before carving. Cut the crackling with a sharp knife, arrange it on a platter with the pork, and serve with the wedges. Delicious with dill coleslaw (see page 330).

Serves 6–8

# Lamb souvlaki roll

1 lb. 2 oz. lamb sirloin
1/2 cup olive oil
3 tablespoons dry white wine
1 tablespoon chopped oregano
3 tablespoons roughly chopped basil
3 garlic cloves, crushed
2 bay leaves, crushed
2 1/2 tablespoons lemon juice
1 large loaf Turkish bread
1 cup baba ghanoush (eggplant dip)
1 tablespoon roughly chopped
    Italian parsley

Place the lamb fillet in a shallow nonmetallic dish. Mix together the oil, wine, oregano, basil, garlic, bay leaves, and 2 tablespoons of the lemon juice and pour over the lamb, turning to coat well. Cover with plastic wrap and marinate for 4 hours.

Remove the lamb fillet from the marinade and cook on a hot, lightly oiled barbecue grill or flat plate for 6–8 minutes or until seared but still pink in the center. Remove from the heat and let rest for 10 minutes, then cut into slices.

Split the Turkish bread lengthwise and spread the bottom thickly with baba ghanoush. Top with the lamb slices, sprinkle with the parsley and remaining lemon juice, then season with salt and pepper. Replace the top of the loaf, then cut into quarters and serve.

Serves 4

# Spicy crab with Singapore-style pepper sauce

4 lb. 8 oz. blue crabs
$3/4$ cup butter
2 tablespoons finely chopped garlic
1 tablespoon finely chopped fresh ginger
1 small red chili, seeded and finely chopped
3 tablespoons ground black pepper
2 tablespoons dark soy sauce
2 tablespoons oyster sauce
1 tablespoon brown sugar
1 scallion, green part only, thinly sliced diagonally

Pull back the apron and remove the top shell from each crab (it should come off in one piece). Remove the intestine and the gray feathery gills, then use a sharp knife to cut the crab in half lengthwise, leaving the legs attached. Crack the thick part of the legs with the back of a heavy knife, or use crab crackers, to make it easier to extract the meat.

Heat a barbecue flat plate or grill to medium–high heat. Cook the crabs for 5–8 minutes on each side or until they turn orange and are cooked through. Heat a wok over medium heat (you'll need to do this on the stovetop if you don't have a wok attachment on your barbecue), and stir-fry the butter, garlic, ginger, chili, and pepper for 30 seconds or until fragrant. Add the combined soy and oyster sauces and sugar and simmer for 1 minute or until glossy.

Toss the cooked crab in the sauce until it is completely coated, then arrange it on a serving dish, sprinkle with the scallions, and serve with steamed rice and a green salad. This dish is very rich and very messy to eat—make sure there are plenty of paper towels or napkins on hand to clean up spills.

Serves 4–6

# Lime and cilantro grilled chicken

3 teaspoons finely grated fresh
  ginger
1/2 cup chopped cilantro
1 1/2 teaspoons grated lime zest
1/3 cup lime juice
4 skinless chicken breast fillets
  (about 1 lb. 10 oz.), trimmed
1 1/4 cups jasmine rice
2 tablespoons vegetable oil
3 zucchini, cut into wedges
4 large flat mushrooms, stalks
  trimmed

Combine the ginger, cilantro, lime zest, and 2 tablespoons of the lime juice. Spread 2 teaspoons of the herb mixture over each fillet and season well. Marinate for 1 hour. Combine the remaining herb mixture with the remaining lime juice in a screw-top jar. Set aside until needed.

Bring a large saucepan of water to a boil. Add the rice and cook for 12 minutes, stirring occasionally. Drain well.

Meanwhile, heat a barbecue plate to medium and lightly brush with oil. Brush the zucchini and mushrooms with the remaining oil. Place the chicken on the grill and cook on each side for 4–5 minutes or until cooked through. Add the vegetables during the last 5 minutes of cooking and turn frequently until browned on the outside and just softened. Cover with foil until ready to serve.

Divide the rice among four serving bowls. Cut the chicken fillets into long, thick strips, then arrange on top of the rice. Shake the dressing well and drizzle over the chicken and serve with the grilled vegetables.

Serves 4

## Lamb stuffed with olives, feta, and oregano

½ cup kalamata olives, pitted
3 garlic cloves, crushed
½ cup olive oil
1 lb. 12 oz. lamb sirloin, trimmed
  (see Note)
3¼ oz. feta cheese, crumbled
2 tablespoons oregano leaves,
  finely shredded
⅓ cup lemon juice

Put the kalamata olives in a food processor or blender with the garlic and 2 tablespoons of olive oil and blend until it is smooth. Season to taste with ground black pepper.

Prepare the sirloin by cutting horizontally most of the way through the piece, starting at one end, and leaving a small joint at the other end. Open out the lamb so you have a piece half as thick and twice as long as you started with.

Spread the olive and garlic paste in a thin, even layer over the cut surface of the lamb, then crumble the feta over the top and sprinkle with the chopped oregano. Roll up the lamb tightly, starting with one of the long cut edges, and tie the whole length with cooking twine so that the filling is contained and secure.

Put the lamb into a dish large enough to hold it lying flat and drizzle it with the lemon juice and remaining olive oil, turning to make sure that all of the lamb is well coated. Cover the dish and refrigerate it for 3 hours.

Preheat a grill to medium–high heat. Season the lamb and grill it for 10 minutes, turning once to brown each side, until it is cooked to your liking. Remove it from the

barbecue and let it rest, covered, for 5 minutes. Use a very sharp knife to cut the roll diagonally into 2-inch pieces and serve it immediately with a mixed green salad.

Serves 4

Note: Use the thick end of the sirloin for this recipe.

## Chili pork ribs

2 lb. 4 oz. pork spareribs
4½-oz. can pureed tomatoes
2 tablespoons honey
2 tablespoons chili sauce
2 tablespoons hoisin sauce
2 tablespoons lime juice
2 garlic cloves, crushed
1 tablespoon vegetable oil

Cut each rib into thirds, then lay them in a single layer in a shallow nonmetallic dish.

Mix together all the other ingredients except the oil and pour over the meat, turning to coat well. Cover with plastic wrap and refrigerate overnight, turning occasionally.

Drain the ribs, reserving the marinade, and cook them over medium heat on a lightly oiled barbecue grill or flat plate. Baste often with the marinade and cook for 15–20 minutes or until the ribs are tender and well browned, turning occasionally. Season to taste and serve immediately.

Serves 4–6

# Grilled haloumi salad

1½ tablespoons lemon juice
2 tablespoons finely chopped
   mint leaves
½ cup olive oil
2 garlic cloves
8 slices ciabatta bread
10½ oz. haloumi cheese, cut into
   ½-inch slices
3 ripe tomatoes
5½ oz. arugula leaves
2 tablespoons pine nuts, toasted

Whisk the lemon juice, mint, ¼ cup of olive oil, and 1 clove of crushed garlic together and season with salt and pepper.

Brush both sides of each slice of bread with 1 tablespoon of olive oil and season well. Brush the haloumi with 1 tablespoon of olive oil. Cut the tomatoes into ½-inch rounds, brush with 1 tablespoon olive oil, and season well.

Preheat a barbecue to medium heat and grill the bread for 1 minute on each side or until it is golden and marked. Rub each piece on both sides with the remaining clove of garlic. Wrap the toast in foil and keep it warm on the side of the barbecue. Grill the haloumi and tomato for 3–5 minutes on each side or until they are browned, then drizzle with 1 tablespoon of the mint and lemon dressing.

Put the arugula and pine nuts in a large bowl, add the remaining dressing, and toss gently until the salad is coated with the dressing. Pile some onto a piece of the garlic toast, arrange some grilled haloumi and tomatoes across the top, and serve it warm.

Serves 4

# Barbecued sardines

8 large fresh sardines
8 sprigs lemon thyme
3 tablespoons extra-virgin olive oil
2 garlic cloves, crushed
1 teaspoon finely grated lemon zest
2 tablespoons lemon juice
1 teaspoon ground cumin
lemon wedges, to serve

Carefully slit the sardines from head to tail and remove the guts. Rinse, then pat dry inside and out with paper towels. Place a sprig of lemon thyme in each fish cavity and arrange the fish in a shallow nonmetallic dish.

Combine the olive oil, garlic, lemon zest, lemon juice, and cumin and pour over the fish. Cover and refrigerate for 2 hours.

Cook the sardines on a hot, lightly oiled barbecue flat plate, basting frequently with the marinade, for about 2–3 minutes each side or until the flesh flakes easily when tested with a fork. Alternatively, barbecue in a sardine cooking rack until tender. Serve hot with lemon wedges.

Serves 4

## Roast lamb

5 lb. 8 oz. leg of lamb
6 garlic cloves, peeled
2 tablespoons rosemary leaves
1 tablespoon olive oil

Make twelve small incisions in the fleshy parts of the lamb. Cut the garlic cloves in half lengthwise and push them into the incisions with the rosemary leaves. Rub the lamb with the oil and season it liberally with salt and pepper. Preheat a covered barbecue to medium indirect heat, put the lamb in the middle of the barbecue, replace the lid, and let it roast for 1 hour 30 minutes.

When the lamb is ready, remove it from the barbecue and let it cool, covered, for 10 minutes before carving and serving it with any juices that have been released while it rested. This dish is sensational with ratatouille (see page 353).

Serves 6

## Stuffed pork chops with grilled scallions

2 tablespoons dry sherry
4 dried dessert figs
1 tablespoon butter
¼ cup olive oil
1 small onion, finely diced
2 garlic cloves, crushed
1 large Granny Smith apple, peeled, cored, and grated
2 tablespoons slivered almonds, lightly toasted
1 tablespoon finely chopped sage leaves
6 large pork loin chops (9 oz. each), on the bone
16 large scallions, green parts removed, halved

Bring the sherry and 1 tablespoon of water to a boil in a small saucepan. Soak the figs in the hot sherry mixture for about 20 minutes, then slice them finely and keep the soaking liquid to use later.

Heat the butter and 1 tablespoon of olive oil in a frying pan, add the onion and garlic, and cook over low heat for 5 minutes or until they are softened. Add the grated apple, figs, and sherry liquid and simmer for another 5 minutes or until the apple has softened and most of the liquid has evaporated. Remove the pan from the heat and stir in the almonds and sage, then season well and allow the mixture to cool.

Trim the pork chops of any excess fat and make an incision into the middle of the chops from the side. Be careful, as you only want to make a pocket in the flesh and not cut right through. Fill the pocket with the apple and fig stuffing, pushing it well into the cavity so that none is spilling out—you should fit about 1 1/2 tablespoons of filling in each chop. Brush the chops all over with 1 tablespoon of the olive oil and season with salt and freshly ground black pepper. Toss the scallions with the remaining oil and season well.

Heat a barbecue grill to medium heat. Cook the chops for 8 minutes on each side or until the outside is slightly charred and the meat is cooked through. While the chops are cooking, add the scallions to the grill and cook them for 10 minutes or until they are softened. Serve the chops and scallions as soon as they are done.

Serves 6

# Jumbo shrimp with dill mayonnaise

*Marinade*
½ cup olive oil
⅓ cup lemon juice
2 tablespoons whole-grain mustard
2 tablespoons honey
2 tablespoons chopped dill

16–20 raw jumbo shrimp

*Dill mayonnaise*
¾ cup mayonnaise
2 tablespoons chopped dill
1½ tablespoons lemon juice
1 gherkin, finely chopped
1 teaspoon chopped capers
1 garlic clove, crushed

To make the marinade, combine the olive oil, lemon juice, mustard, honey, and dill, pour over the unpeeled shrimp, and coat well. Cover and refrigerate for at least 2 hours, turning occasionally.

To make the dill mayonnaise, whisk together the mayonnaise, dill, lemon juice, gherkin, capers, and garlic. Cover and refrigerate.

Cook the drained shrimp on a hot, lightly oiled barbecue grill or flat plate in batches for 4 minutes, turning frequently until pink and cooked through. Serve with the mayonnaise.

Serves 4

## Beef with blue-cheese butter

7 tablespoons butter, softened
2 garlic cloves, crushed
3½ oz. Blue Castello or other
  blue cheese
2 teaspoons finely shredded sage
  leaves
2 lb. 4 oz. beef eye fillet (thick end),
  trimmed
1 tablespoon olive oil

To make the blue-cheese butter, mash together the softened butter, garlic, cheese, and sage until they are well combined. Form the mixture into a log and wrap it in waxed paper, twisting the ends to seal them. Refrigerate the butter until firm, then cut it into ¼-inch slices and leave it at room temperature until needed.

Cut the beef into four thick, equal pieces and tie a piece of string around the edge of each so it will keep its shape during cooking. Brush both sides of each steak with the oil and season with freshly ground pepper. Heat a barbecue to medium–high heat and cook the beef on the grill for 6–7 minutes each side for medium or until done to your liking.

Put two slices of blue-cheese butter on top of each steak as soon as you remove it from the barbecue and remove the string. This is delicious served with pear and walnut salad (see page 297).

Serves 4

Note: Any leftover butter can be wrapped in waxed paper and foil and frozen for up to 2 months. It is also delicious with chicken and pork.

# Chicken Caesar salad

*Caesar dressing*
1 egg yolk
1 garlic clove, crushed
3 anchovy fillets
1 teaspoon Dijon mustard
1/2 cup vegetable oil
1 tablespoon lemon juice
1/2 teaspoon Worcestershire
  sauce
2 teaspoons grated Parmesan cheese

4 chicken thigh fillets, trimmed
  of fat and sinew
1/3 cup olive oil
12 baguette slices, 1/2 inch thick
1 garlic clove, halved
4 slices bacon
2 heads romaine lettuce, washed
  well and drained
extra anchovies, optional

Put the egg yolk, garlic, anchovies, and mustard in a food processor and blend them together. With the motor running, gradually add the oil in a thin stream and process until the mixture becomes thick. Stir in the lemon juice, Worcestershire sauce, and Parmesan and season with salt and pepper. Put the chicken thighs in a bowl with 1 tablespoon of olive oil, season to taste, and turn to coat well with oil.

Preheat a barbecue grill to medium–high heat. Brush the baguette slices with the remaining olive oil and toast on the grill for 1 minute each side or until they are crisp and marked. Rub both sides of each piece of toast with the cut clove of garlic and keep warm.

Grill the chicken on the grill for 5 minutes on each side or until cooked through. Leave to cool for 1 minute, then cut into 1/2-inch strips. Cook the bacon for 3 minutes each side or until crispy, then break into 3/4-inch pieces.

Tear the lettuce leaves into bite-size pieces and toss them in a large bowl with the dressing, bacon, and chicken. Serve with the garlic croutons and let people add extra anchovies to taste.

Serves 4–6

# Lamb fillets wrapped in vine leaves with avgolemono sauce

12 lamb fillets (approximately
  1 lb. 9 oz. total)
2 teaspoons lemon juice
1½ teaspoons ground cumin
2 tablespoons olive oil
2 lb. 4 oz. (about 6 medium) waxy
  potatoes (e.g., pink fir apple, red)
12 large vine leaves preserved
  in brine

*Avgolemono sauce*
2 eggs
1 egg yolk
¼ cup lemon juice
4 cups chicken stock

Trim the fillets and put them in a bowl with the lemon juice, cumin, and 1 tablespoon of the olive oil, then turn the fillets so they are coated. Cover the bowl and leave the lamb to marinate for 1 hour. Steam or boil the potatoes for 10–15 minutes or until they are just tender. When they are cool enough to handle, peel them and slice each one in half lengthwise. Toss the potato halves gently in the remaining olive oil and season with salt and pepper.

Rinse the vine leaves under warm water, pat dry with paper towels, and remove any woody stems. Lay the leaf flat with the vein side facing up, remove the lamb from the marinade, season it well with salt and pepper, and put a lamb fillet on the bottom of each vine leaf. Roll up the leaf so that it is wrapped around the lamb with the joint sitting underneath.

To make the avgolemono sauce, whisk the whole eggs, egg yolk, and lemon juice together, then bring the chicken stock to a boil and add 1 tablespoon of the hot stock to the egg mixture. Mix them together, then slowly add the egg mixture to the stock, stirring continuously. Cook the sauce over low heat, stirring it constantly with a wooden spoon for 4–5 minutes or until it thickens enough to hold a line drawn across the back of the spoon. Be careful not to let the sauce boil, or the mixture will curdle.

Preheat a barbecue to medium heat. Cook the potatoes on the grill for 6–7 minutes or until they are golden and crisp and the lamb fillets for 1–2 minutes on each side for medium–rare or until they are done to your liking.

Slice the lamb fillets in half diagonally and serve them with the sauce and grilled potatoes.

Serves 4

# Scallops with sesame bok choy

24 large scallops with corals
2 tablespoons light soy sauce
1 tablespoon fish sauce
1 tablespoon honey
1 tablespoon kecap manis
grated zest and juice of 1 lime
2 teaspoons grated fresh ginger
lime wedges, to serve

*Sesame bok choy*
1 tablespoon sesame oil
1 tablespoon sesame seeds
1 garlic clove, crushed
8 baby bok choy, halved lengthwise

Rinse the scallops, remove the dark vein, and dry with paper towels. Mix the soy and fish sauces, honey, kecap manis, lime zest and juice, and ginger. Pour over the scallops, cover, and refrigerate for 15 minutes. Drain, reserving the marinade.

To make the sesame bok choy, pour the oil onto a hot barbecue flat plate and add the sesame seeds and garlic. Cook, stirring, for 1 minute or until the seeds are golden. Arrange the bok choy in a single layer on the hot plate and pour the reserved marinade on top. Cook for 3–4 minutes, turning once, until tender. Remove and keep warm.

Wipe clean the flat plate, brush with oil, and reheat. Add the scallops and cook, turning, for about 2 minutes or until they become opaque. Serve on top of the bok choy with the lime wedges.

Serves 4

# Chili bean tortilla wraps

*Chili beans*
2 tablespoons olive oil
2 garlic cloves, crushed
1 onion, finely chopped
1 green pepper, seeded, cored, and chopped
2 small red chilies, seeded and finely chopped
1/2 teaspoon cayenne pepper
1 teaspoon paprika
1 teaspoon ground cumin
1/4 teaspoon sugar
15-oz. can crushed tomatoes
15-oz. can red kidney beans, drained and rinsed
1 tablespoon tomato paste

12 (8-inch) soft flour tortillas
2 cups shredded cheddar cheese
1 cup sour cream
cilantro, to garnish
1 lime, cut into 8 wedges

To make the chili beans, heat the oil in a saucepan over low heat and cook the garlic, onion, and pepper, stirring frequently, for 8–10 minutes or until the onion and pepper have softened. Add the chili, cayenne pepper, paprika, cumin, sugar, tomato, beans, tomato paste, and 1/2 cup water. Bring the mixture to a boil, then reduce the heat and simmer for 15–20 minutes or until it is thickened and reduced. Season to taste.

To assemble the wraps, put some of the chili beans along the middle of each tortilla, sprinkle with 2 tablespoons of the cheese, and roll it up. Put three rolls, seam-side down, on a double layer of foil and seal the foil to form a parcel. Preheat a barbecue flat plate to low–medium heat and grill the parcels for 6–8 minutes on each side or until they are heated through.

Unwrap the foil parcels and slide the tortillas onto serving plates. Top them with the sour cream, garnish with cilantro, and serve with the lime wedges. Even better, add some guacamole (see page 334) and tomato salsa (see page 342).

Serves 4

# Lebanese chicken

1 cup plain yogurt
2 teaspoons brown sugar
4 garlic cloves, crushed
3 teaspoons ground cumin
1 1/2 teaspoons ground coriander
1/4 cup chopped Italian parsley
1/4 cup lemon juice
1 (4-lb.) whole chicken, cut into
   10 serving pieces
vegetable oil spray

Put the yogurt, brown sugar, garlic, cumin, coriander, chopped parsley, and lemon juice in a large nonmetallic bowl and mix them together. Add the chicken pieces to the marinade and turn them so that they are completely coated, then cover and refrigerate for at least 2 hours or overnight.

Lightly spray the barbecue plates with oil, then preheat the barbecue to medium heat. Take the chicken pieces out of the marinade and season them with salt and pepper. Cook the chicken pieces on the flat plate, turning them frequently, for 20–30 minutes or until they are cooked through. If you have a barbecue with a lid, cover the barbecue while the chicken is cooking. This way, the breast pieces will take only 15 minutes to cook, while the pieces on the bone will take about 10 minutes longer. This dish is delicious served with eggplant, tomato, and sumac salad (see page 301).

Serves 4–6

# Pork with apple and onion wedges

2 pork fillets, about 14 oz. each
12 pitted prunes
2 green apples, cored, unpeeled,
  and cut into wedges
2 red onions, cut into wedges
4 tablespoons butter, melted
2 teaspoons superfine sugar
1/2 cup cream
2 tablespoons brandy
1 tablespoon chopped chives

Trim the pork of any excess fat and sinew and cut each fillet in half. Make a slit with a knife through the center of each fillet and push three prunes into each one. Brush the pork and the apple and onion wedges with the melted butter and sprinkle the apple and onion with the sugar.

Brown the pork on a hot, lightly oiled barbecue flat plate. Add the apple and onion wedges (you may need to cook in batches if your flat plate isn't large enough). Cook, turning frequently, for 5–7 minutes or until the pork is cooked through and the apple and onion pieces are softened. Remove the pork, apples, and onions from the barbecue and keep warm.

Mix together the cream, brandy, and chives in a pan. Transfer to the stovetop and simmer for 3 minutes or until slightly thickened. Season with salt and black pepper.

Slice the meat and serve with the apple and onion wedges and brandy cream sauce.

Serves 4

## Margarita chicken

4 chicken breasts, skins left on,
    tenderloin and any excess fat
    removed
¼ cup tequila
¼ cup lime juice
2 small chilies, finely chopped
3 garlic cloves, crushed
¼ cup finely chopped cilantro
1 tablespoon olive oil
lime wedges, to serve

Put the chicken, tequila, lime juice, chili, garlic, cilantro, and olive oil in a nonmetallic bowl and mix it all together so that the chicken is coated in the marinade. Cover the bowl and refrigerate for at least 2 hours or preferably overnight.

Preheat a barbecue grill to medium–high heat. Remove the chicken breasts from the marinade, season them with salt and pepper, and grill for 7–8 minutes on each side or until they are cooked through.

Slice the chicken breasts diagonally and serve with lime wedges. Delicious with avocado and grapefruit salad (see page 322).

Serves 4

# Rosemary and red wine steaks with barbecued vegetables

12 small new potatoes
¼ cup olive oil
1 tablespoon finely chopped rosemary
6 garlic cloves, sliced
sea salt, to season
4 large, thick mushrooms
12 asparagus spears
1 cup red wine
4 steak fillets, about 9 oz. each

Heat a barbecue plate or grill until hot. Toss the potatoes with 1 tablespoon of oil, half the rosemary, and half the garlic and season with the sea salt. Divide the potatoes among four large sheets of foil and wrap up into neat packages, sealing firmly around the edges. Place on the barbecue and cook, turning frequently, for 30–40 minutes or until tender. Meanwhile, brush the mushrooms and asparagus with a little oil and set aside.

Put the wine, remaining oil, rosemary, and garlic in a nonmetallic dish and season with pepper. Add the steaks and turn to coat well in the marinade. Leave for 25 minutes, then drain.

Place the steaks on the barbecue with the mushrooms and cook for 4 minutes each side or until cooked to your liking. Transfer the steaks and mushrooms to a plate, cover lightly, and allow to cool. Add the asparagus to the barbecue, turning regularly for about 2 minutes or until tender. By this stage your potatoes should be cooked—open the foil and pierce with a skewer to check for doneness. Season with salt and pepper. Serve each steak with a mushroom, three asparagus spears, and a package of potatoes.

Serves 4

## Spanish-style seafood salad with romesco sauce

8 raw slipper lobsters
2 lb. 4 oz. raw jumbo shrimp
1 lb. 2 oz. baby squid tubes, cleaned
½ cup olive oil
3 garlic cloves, finely chopped
¼ cup chopped basil
⅓ cup lemon juice
5½ oz. arugula leaves
5½ oz. curly endive
2 tablespoons extra-virgin olive oil
1 tablespoon red wine vinegar

*Romesco sauce*
⅓ cup olive oil
¼ teaspoon paprika
1 small red pepper, seeded and
    quartered lengthwise
3 ripe Roma tomatoes
2 long red chilies
⅓ cup blanched almonds and
    hazelnuts, toasted
3 garlic cloves, crushed
1 tablespoon red wine vinegar
1 tablespoon lemon juice

To prepare the lobsters, cut into the membrane where the head and body join, then twist off the tail and discard the head. Use kitchen scissors to cut down both sides of the underside shell, working the scissors between the flesh and shell, then peel back the undershell and throw it away. Remove the heads and legs from the shrimp, leaving the shells and tails intact. Turn each shrimp on its back and cut a slit through the center lengthwise, being careful not to cut all the way through. Open out the shrimp to form a butterfly and remove the dark vein from the back, starting at the head end. Wash the squid and pat them dry with paper towels, then cut a small slit in the base of the tubes so that they open up when cooking.

Mix together the oil, garlic, basil, and lemon juice in a large bowl, add the seafood, and toss so that it is well coated. Cover and chill for 30 minutes.

To make the romesco sauce, preheat a barbecue to medium heat. Mix half the olive oil with the paprika, add the pepper, tomatoes, and chilies, and toss. Cook the pepper and tomatoes on the grill for 5 minutes, then add the chilies and cook for another 5 minutes or until the tomatoes are soft and the vegetables are charred. Peel the pepper and tomatoes when they are cool, then remove the seeds and skin from the chili. Process the nuts until they are finely ground. Add the vegetables, garlic, vinegar, and juice and blend to a paste. Slowly add the remaining oil and season to taste. If the sauce is too thick, add 2 tablespoons of water to get it to a pouring consistency.

Toss the salad leaves with the olive oil and vinegar, cover, and refrigerate.

Heat the grill to very high heat. Cook the lobsters for 5–6 minutes or until the shells turn pink and the flesh starts pulling away from the shells. Halfway through cooking the lobsters, add the shrimp and cook them, flesh-side down, for 2–3 minutes. Turn and cook for another 2–3 minutes or until pink and cooked through. Add the squid after turning the shrimp and cook for 1–2 minutes or until they are brown, marked, and just cooked through. Remove all of the seafood from the barbecue as soon as it is just done, as residual heat will continue to cook it. Arrange the salad leaves on a plate, top with the seafood, and drizzle with the romesco sauce. Serve at once, with any remaining romesco sauce and bread rolls to soak up the juices.

Serves 4

## Lamb chops with citrus pockets

4 lamb chops, about 9 oz. each
2 tablespoons lemon juice

*Citrus filling*
3 scallions, finely chopped
1 celery stalk, finely chopped
2 teaspoons grated fresh ginger
3/4 cup fresh bread crumbs
2 tablespoons orange juice
2 teaspoons finely grated orange zest
1 teaspoon chopped rosemary

Cut a deep, long pocket in the side of each lamb chop. Mix together the scallions, celery, ginger, bread crumbs, orange juice, zest, and rosemary and spoon into the pockets in the lamb.

Cook on a hot, lightly oiled barbecue flat plate or grill, turning once, for 15 minutes or until the lamb is cooked through but still pink in the center. Drizzle with the lemon juice before serving.

Serves 4

# Five-spice roast chicken

4-lb. whole chicken
1 tablespoon soy sauce
2 garlic cloves, crushed
1 teaspoon finely grated
   fresh ginger
1 tablespoon honey
1 tablespoon rice wine
1 teaspoon five-spice powder
1 tablespoon peanut oil

Wash the chicken and pat it thoroughly dry inside and out with paper towels. Whisk the soy sauce, garlic, ginger, honey, rice wine, and five-spice powder together in a small bowl and brush it all over the chicken, making sure every bit of skin is well coated. Put the chicken on a wire rack over a baking tray and refrigerate it, uncovered, for at least 8 hours or overnight.

Preheat a covered barbecue to medium indirect heat and put a drip tray under the rack. Brush the chicken liberally with the peanut oil and put it breast-side up in the middle of the barbecue over the drip tray. Cover the barbecue and roast the chicken for 1 hour 10 minutes or until the juices run clear when you pierce it with a skewer between the thigh and body. Check the chicken every so often, and if it appears to be browning too much, cover it loosely with foil. Leave it to cool, covered, for 10 minutes before carving and serving. The flavors in this style of chicken go particularly well with steamed Asian greens and fried rice.

Serves 4

# Sweet chili octopus

3 lb. 5 oz. baby octopus
1 cup sweet chili sauce
$\frac{1}{3}$ cup lime juice
$\frac{1}{3}$ cup fish sauce
$\frac{1}{3}$ cup brown sugar
lime wedges, to serve

Cut off the octopus heads, below the eyes, with a sharp knife. Discard the heads and guts. Push the beaks out with your index finger, remove, and discard. Wash the octopus thoroughly under running water and drain on crumpled paper towels. If the octopus tentacles are large, cut into quarters.

Mix together the sweet chili sauce, lime juice, fish sauce, and sugar.

Cook the octopus on a very hot, lightly oiled barbecue grill or flat plate, turning often, for 3–4 minutes or until it just changes color. Brush with a quarter of the sauce during cooking. Be careful not to overcook the octopus or it will toughen. Serve immediately with the remaining sauce and lime wedges.

Serves 4

## Sesame and ginger beef

¼ cup sesame oil
¼ cup soy sauce
2 garlic cloves, crushed
2 tablespoons grated fresh ginger
1 tablespoon lemon juice
2 tablespoons chopped scallions
⅓ cup brown sugar
1 lb. 2 oz. beef fillet

Combine the sesame oil, soy sauce, garlic, ginger, lemon juice, scallions, and brown sugar in a nonmetallic dish. Add the beef and coat well with the marinade. Cover and refrigerate for at least 2 hours or overnight if possible.

Brown the beef on all sides on a very hot, lightly oiled barbecue grill or flat plate. When the beef is sealed, remove, wrap in foil, and return to the barbecue, turning occasionally, for another 15–20 minutes, depending on how well done you like your meat. Leave for 10 minutes before slicing.

Put the leftover marinade in a small saucepan and boil for 5 minutes. This is delicious served as a sauce with the beef.

Serves 4–6

# Lobster with burned butter sauce and grilled lemon

3/4 cup butter
1/4 cup lemon juice
2 tablespoons chopped Italian parsley
1 small garlic clove, crushed
8 lobster tails in the shell
2 lemons, cut into wedges

Melt the butter in a small saucepan over medium heat and cook it for 3 minutes or until it begins to brown, but watch it carefully to make sure that it doesn't burn. Lower the heat and cook the butter for another 2 minutes or until it is a dark, golden brown. Remove the pan from the heat, add the lemon juice, parsley, and garlic, and season with salt and freshly ground black pepper.

Cut the lobster tails lengthwise and remove any digestive tract, but leave the meat in the shell. Preheat a barbecue grill to medium heat and brush the exposed lobster meat with lots of the butter mixture. Cook the lobster tails, cut-side down, on the grill for 6 minutes, then turn them over and cook for another 3–5 minutes or until the shells turn bright red. While the lobster is cooking, put the lemon wedges on the hottest part of the grill and cook them for 1 minute on each side or until they are marked and heated through. Arrange the lobster on a serving plate and serve with the grilled lemon wedges and the rest of the warm brown butter as a dipping sauce. This is delicious with a green salad and some crusty bread to soak up the juices.

Serves 8

## Lamb kofta with baba ghanoush and grilled olives

*Kofta*

1 red onion, finely chopped
3/4 cup chopped Italian parsley
1/2 cup chopped cilantro
1/4 cup chopped mint leaves
1 tablespoon paprika
1 tablespoon ground cumin
1 1/2 teaspoons allspice
1/2 teaspoon ground ginger
1/2 teaspoon chili flakes
2 lb. 11 oz. ground lamb
1/4 cup soda water

*Baba ghanoush*

2 eggplants, 1 lb. 12 oz. each
2 garlic cloves, finely chopped
1/4 teaspoon ground cumin
1/4 cup lemon juice
2–2 1/2 tablespoons tahini
1/4 cup olive oil

1 tablespoon chopped Italian parsley
1/2 teaspoon sumac
1 cup kalamata olives
olive oil, for brushing
4 pieces pita bread

To make the kofta, put the onion, parsley, cilantro, mint, paprika, cumin, allspice, ginger, and chili in a food processor and blend until they are combined. Season the mixture with 2 teaspoons salt and some freshly ground black pepper, then add the ground lamb to the food processor and get the motor going again. Add the soda water in a thin stream until the mixture forms a smooth paste, then cover and refrigerate for at least 2 hours or preferably overnight.

To make the baba ghanoush, preheat a covered barbecue grill to medium–high. Prick the eggplants a few times with a fork and cook them, covered, for 20 minutes or until they are soft and wrinkled, turning them halfway through the cooking time. Put the eggplants in a colander and leave them for 30 minutes to allow any bitter juices to drain, then peel and discard the skin and roughly chop the flesh. Put the eggplant in a food processor with the garlic, cumin, lemon juice, tahini, and olive oil and process the baba ghanoush for 30 seconds or until it is smooth and creamy. Season to taste with salt, then cover and refrigerate. Sprinkle the baba ghanoush with the parsley and sumac before serving.

Soak four wooden skewers in cold water for 1 hour. Divide the lamb mixture into twelve portions and mold each portion into a torpedo shape, using damp hands to keep the meat from sticking to your hands, then cover and refrigerate the kofta. Thread the olives onto the soaked skewers.

When you're ready to cook the kofta, preheat a barbecue flat plate to medium–high heat. Brush the kofta lightly with olive oil and cook, turning frequently, for 10–12 minutes or until they are evenly browned and cooked through. When the kofta are nearly cooked, add the olives to the barbecue for 1–2 minutes. Serve the kofta immediately with pita bread, the baba ghanoush, and grilled olives. Tabbouleh (see page 305) makes a delicious accompaniment to this meal.

Serves 4

# Spicy buffalo wings with ranch dressing

12 large chicken wings
2 teaspoons garlic salt
2 teaspoons onion powder
vegetable oil, for deep-frying
1/2 cup tomato sauce
2 tablespoons Worcestershire
  sauce
4 tablespoons butter, melted
hot pepper sauce, to taste

*Ranch dressing*
1 small garlic clove, crushed
3/4 cup mayonnaise
1/2 cup buttermilk
2 tablespoons finely chopped
  Italian parsley
1 tablespoon finely chopped
  chives
1 1/2 teaspoons lemon juice
1 1/2 teaspoons Dijon mustard
1 teaspoon onion powder

Pat the wings dry with paper towels, remove and discard the tip of each wing, then cut them in half at the joint. Combine the garlic salt, onion powder, and 2 teaspoons of ground black pepper and rub the spice mixture into each chicken piece.

Deep-fry the chicken in batches for 2–3 minutes without letting it brown, then remove from the oil and drain on crumpled paper towels. When the chicken has cooled a little, put it in a nonmetallic bowl with the combined tomato sauce, Worcestershire sauce, butter, and hot pepper sauce and toss so that all of the pieces are well coated in the marinade. Cover and refrigerate for at least 2 hours or overnight.

To make the ranch dressing, mash the garlic and 1/4 teaspoon salt to a paste, then add the mayonnaise, buttermilk, parsley, chives, lemon juice, mustard, and onion powder and whisk it all together. Season well, cover, and chill for at least 1 hour before serving.

Preheat a barbecue to medium heat. Cook the chicken for 6–8 minutes on each side or until it is caramelized and sticky, turning and basting with the marinade as it cooks. Serve hot with the ranch dressing.

Serves 4

# Adobo pork with coconut rice

2/3 cup balsamic vinegar
1/3 cup soy sauce
3 fresh bay leaves
4 garlic cloves, crushed
6 pork loin chops on the bone
2 tablespoons vegetable oil
lime wedges, to serve

*Coconut rice*
2 cups jasmine rice
2 tablespoons vegetable oil
1 small onion, finely diced
1 teaspoon grated fresh ginger
2 garlic cloves, crushed
2½ cups coconut milk

Put the balsamic vinegar, soy sauce, bay leaves, garlic, and ½ teaspoon ground black pepper in a nonmetallic dish and mix them all together. Add the pork chops to the marinade and turn them a few times so that they are thoroughly coated. Cover and chill for at least 3 hours or overnight.

To make the coconut rice, rinse the rice under cold running water until the water runs clear. Heat the oil in a heavy-based saucepan over medium heat, then add the onion, ginger, and garlic. Cook for 3 minutes or until the onion has softened, then add the rice and stir until the rice is coated in oil. Stir in the coconut milk, bring it to a boil, then turn the heat down as low as possible and cook it very gently, covered, for 15 minutes. Remove from the heat and let the rice sit with the lid on for 5 minutes before gently fluffing it with a fork. Season well.

Preheat a barbecue grill to medium heat. Remove the pork from the marinade and pat it dry with paper towels. Brush both sides of the chops with oil, season, and cook for 8 minutes each side or until cooked through. Serve with the coconut rice and lime wedges. Delicious with grilled mangoes (see page 298).

Serves 6

## Chicken with salsa verde

1 garlic clove
2 cups fresh Italian parsley
1/3 cup extra-virgin olive oil
3 tablespoons chopped dill
1 1/2 tablespoons Dijon mustard
1 tablespoon sherry vinegar
1 tablespoon baby capers, drained
6 large chicken breast fillets

Place the garlic, parsley, olive oil, dill, mustard, vinegar, and capers in a food processor or blender and process until almost smooth.

Cook the chicken fillets on a very hot, lightly oiled barbecue grill or flat plate for 4–5 minutes each side or until cooked through.

Cut each chicken fillet diagonally into three pieces and arrange on serving plates. Top with a spoonful of salsa verde and season to taste.

Serves 6

## Korean barbecue beef in lettuce leaves

1 lb. 5 oz. sirloin steak
1 onion, grated
5 garlic cloves, crushed
½ cup soy sauce
1 teaspoon sesame oil
1 tablespoon vegetable oil
2 teaspoons finely grated fresh ginger
2 tablespoons brown sugar
1 tablespoon toasted sesame seeds, ground
1 head butter lettuce
2 cups cooked white rice
2 scallions, finely sliced diagonally
2 small red chilies, sliced, or chili sauce, optional

Trim any excess fat from the steak, then put it in the freezer for about 45 minutes or until it is almost frozen through. Put the onion, garlic, soy sauce, oils, ginger, sugar, ground sesame seeds, and 1 teaspoon of freshly ground black pepper in a large nonmetallic bowl and stir it all together well.

Using a very sharp, heavy knife, cut the steak across the grain into $1/8$-inch-thick slices. Use a meat mallet or rolling pin to pound the meat until it is as thin as possible. Add the meat to the marinade and stir it to make sure that all of the meat is well coated in the marinade. Cover and refrigerate overnight.

Separate the lettuce leaves and put them in a large bowl with enough cold water to cover them, then refrigerate until ready to serve.

When you are ready to start cooking, remove the meat and the lettuce from the refrigerator and drain the lettuce well or dry it in a salad spinner. Put the lettuce leaves, hot rice, scallions, and chili in separate bowls and put them on the table so each person can serve themselves. Preheat the flat plate to high indirect heat, and working quickly, put the beef strips on the flat plate, spacing them out in

a single layer, and cook them for about 10 seconds on each side. Do this in two batches if your barbecue isn't large enough to hold them all at once.

To make a wrap, put some rice in the bottom of a lettuce leaf, top it with a little meat, some scallions, and chili if desired, then wrap the leaf around the filling.

Serves 4–6

# Squid with picada dressing

1 lb. 2 oz. small squid

*Picada dressing*
2 tablespoons extra-virgin olive oil
2 tablespoons finely chopped Italian
  parsley
1 garlic clove, crushed
1/4 teaspoon cracked black pepper

To clean the squid, gently pull the tentacles away from the hood (the intestines should come away at the same time). Remove the intestines from the tentacles by cutting under the eyes, then remove the beak (if it remains in the center of the tentacles) by pushing up with your index finger. Pull away the soft bone.

Rub the hoods under cold running water and the skin should come away easily. Wash the hoods and tentacles and drain well. Place in a bowl, add 1/4 teaspoon salt, and mix well. Cover and refrigerate for about 30 minutes.

For the picada dressing, whisk together the olive oil, parsley, garlic, pepper, and some salt.

Cook the squid hoods in small batches on a very hot, lightly oiled barbecue flat plate for 2–3 minutes or until white and tender. Grill the tentacles, turning to brown them all over, for 1 minute or until they curl up. Serve hot, drizzled with the picada dressing.

Serves 6

## Tandoori lamb with tomato and onion salsa

¼ cup tandoori paste
1 cup thick plain yogurt
1 tablespoon lemon juice
4 racks of lamb with 4–5 cutlets
  in each

*Tomato and onion salsa*
6 Roma tomatoes
1 red onion
2 tablespoons lemon juice
1 teaspoon sugar
2 tablespoons olive oil

Mix together the tandoori paste, yogurt, and lemon juice in a large nonmetallic bowl. Trim any excess fat off the racks of lamb, add them to the marinade, and turn them so that they are well coated. Cover and refrigerate for at least 4 hours or overnight.

To make the tomato and onion salsa, cut the tomatoes into thin wedges, slice the onion very thinly, and toss them both with the lemon juice, sugar, and olive oil. Season the salsa with salt and lots of ground black pepper.

Preheat a covered barbecue to medium–high indirect heat. Cook the lamb, covered, for 10 minutes, then turn it, baste with the marinade, and cook it for another 8 minutes. Leave it to cool, covered with foil, for 5 minutes. Serve the racks whole or sliced with the tomato salsa. This is delicious with minted potato salad (see page 326).

Serves 4

## Drumsticks in tomato and mango chutney

8 chicken drumsticks, scored
1 tablespoon mustard powder
2 tablespoons tomato sauce
1 tablespoon sweet mango chutney
1 teaspoon Worcestershire sauce
1 tablespoon Dijon mustard
¼ cup raisins
1 tablespoon vegetable oil

Toss the chicken in the mustard powder and season with salt and ground black pepper. Combine the tomato sauce, mango chutney, Worcestershire sauce, mustard, raisins, and oil. Spoon over the chicken and toss well. Marinate for at least 2 hours, turning once.

Cook the chicken on a hot, lightly oiled barbecue flat plate for about 20 minutes or until cooked through.

Serves 4

# Smoked trout with lemon and dill butter

*Lemon and dill butter*
½ cup butter, softened
2 tablespoons lemon juice
2 tablespoons finely chopped dill
½ teaspoon lemon zest
1 small garlic clove, crushed

6 hickory wood chips
4 rainbow trout
vegetable oil, for brushing

Mash together the butter, lemon juice, dill, zest, and garlic, shape it into a log, and wrap it in waxed paper, twisting the ends to seal them. Refrigerate the butter until it is firm, then cut it into ½-inch slices and leave it at room temperature.

Preheat a barbecue to low indirect heat, allow the coals to burn down to ashes, then add three hickory wood chips to each side.

Brush the skin of the fish with oil. When the wood chips begin to smoke, put the trout on the barbecue, replace the cover, and smoke them for 15 minutes or until they are cooked through. Remove the fish from the grill, gently peel off the skin, and top them with the lemon and dill butter while they are still hot. Smoked trout are delicious with boiled new potatoes and a green salad, and can also be served cold.

Serves 4

Note: Like barbecuing, smoking is a simple process with a delicious result. Special wood chips are commercially available and give off a wonderfully scented smoke and infuse your food with a distinctive flavor. Never use wood that is not specifically intended for smoking food, as many woods are chemically treated and may release toxins into the food. To smoke food, soak six wood chips in water for 1 hour and prepare a barbecue for indirect cooking. When the briquettes are ready, add three wood chips to each side and close the lid until the chips begin to smoke, then cook the food according to the recipe, lifting the lid as little as possible so you don't lose too much of the smoke. Smoking does not work in a gas or electric barbecue, as the chips need to burn to infuse their aromatic flavor.

# Marinated vegetable salad with bocconcini and pesto dressing

2 large red peppers, cored and seeded
5 slender eggplants, cut diagonally into ½-inch slices
10½ oz. asparagus spears, trimmed and halved
4 zucchini, cut diagonally into ½-inch slices
1 cup small field mushrooms, quartered
½ cup olive oil
4 garlic cloves, crushed
7 oz. bocconcini cheese, sliced
5½ oz. arugula leaves
1 tablespoon balsamic vinegar

*Pesto*
2 cups small basil leaves
⅓ cup pine nuts, toasted
3 garlic cloves, crushed
½ teaspoon sea salt
½ cup olive oil
1 tablespoon Parmesan cheese, finely grated
1 tablespoon pecorino cheese, finely grated

Cut the peppers into quarters, then cut each quarter into three strips. Put the peppers, eggplant, asparagus, zucchini, and mushrooms in a large bowl, pour in the combined oil and garlic, season with salt and freshly ground pepper, and toss it all together. Leave the vegetables to marinate for 1 hour, tossing occasionally.

To make the pesto, put the basil, pine nuts, garlic, salt, and oil in a food processor and process until it is smooth. Stir in the Parmesan and pecorino, then cover the bowl until you are ready to use it.

Heat a barbecue flat plate to high and cook the vegetables, turning, for about 7–8 minutes or until they are soft and golden. Arrange the grilled vegetables on a serving plate with the bocconcini and toss the arugula with the vinegar. Drizzle the vegetables with the pesto and serve them immediately with warm, crusty bread rolls.

Serves 4

## Thai spiced chicken with potato rosti

1 lb. 5 oz. chicken breast fillet, cut into strips
1 tablespoon chopped lemongrass
2 tablespoons lime juice
1½ tablespoons vegetable oil
2 garlic cloves, crushed
1 tablespoon grated fresh ginger
2 teaspoons sweet chili sauce
2 scallions, chopped
1 lime, cut into 6 wedges

*Potato rosti*
1 lb. 5 oz. (about 4 medium) potatoes
3 tablespoons all-purpose flour
1 egg, lightly beaten

Remove any excess fat or sinew from the chicken and put the chicken in a shallow nonmetallic dish. Mix together the lemongrass, lime juice, oil, garlic, ginger, sweet chili sauce, and scallions. Pour over the chicken pieces, cover, and refrigerate for at least 2 hours.

To make the potato rosti, peel and grate the potatoes. Squeeze the excess moisture from the potatoes with your hands until they feel dry. Mix the potatoes with the flour and egg and season well. Divide into six equal portions. Cook on a hot, lightly oiled barbecue flat plate for 10 minutes or until golden brown on both sides, flattening them down with the back of a spatula during cooking.

Drain the chicken and reserve the marinade. Cook on a barbecue grill or flat plate for 3 minutes each side or until tender and golden brown. Brush with the reserved marinade while cooking. Serve with the rosti and a squeeze of lime juice.

Serves 6

## Tuna steaks on cilantro noodles

¼ cup lime juice
2 tablespoons fish sauce
2 tablespoons sweet chili sauce
2 teaspoons brown sugar
1 teaspoon sesame oil
1 garlic clove, finely chopped
1 tablespoon virgin olive oil
4 tuna steaks (5½ oz. each), at
  room temperature
7 oz. spaghettini
6 scallions, thinly sliced
¾ cup chopped cilantro
lime wedges, to garnish

To make the dressing, place the lime juice, fish sauce, chili sauce, sugar, sesame oil, and garlic in a small bowl and mix together.

Heat the olive oil on a barbecue grill. Add the tuna steaks and cook over high heat for 2 minutes each side or until cooked to your liking. Transfer the steaks to a warm plate, cover, and keep warm.

Put the noodles in a large saucepan of lightly salted, boiling water and return to a boil. Cook for 4 minutes or until the noodles are tender. Drain well. Add half the dressing and half the scallions and cilantro to the noodles and gently toss together.

Cut the tuna into even-size cubes or slices.

Place the noodles on serving plates and top with the tuna. Mix the remaining dressing with the scallions and cilantro and drizzle over the tuna. Garnish with lime wedges.

Serves 4

## Roast sirloin with mustard pepper crust and hasselback potatoes

⅓ cup Dijon mustard
2 tablespoons light soy sauce
2 tablespoons all-purpose flour
¼ cup olive oil
3 teaspoons chopped thyme leaves
4 garlic cloves, crushed
5 lb. 8 oz. piece of sirloin, trimmed
  but with the fat still on top
6 russet potatoes
2 tablespoons butter, melted
1 onion, roughly diced
1 large carrot, roughly diced
2 celery stalks, roughly chopped
1 cup red wine
2 cups beef stock
2 bay leaves
2 teaspoons cornstarch

Mix the mustard, soy sauce, flour, 2 tablespoons oil, 2 teaspoons thyme, two of the crushed garlic cloves, and 1 tablespoon cracked black pepper in a small bowl.

Coat the sirloin with the mustard mixture, put it on a wire rack over a tray, and refrigerate it for 1 hour so the crust sets.

To make the hasselback potatoes, boil the potatoes in their skins for 10–12 minutes or until they are just cooked. Once they are cool enough to handle, peel and cut them in half lengthwise. Make small, even slices across the top of the potatoes, cutting only two-thirds of the way down. Brush each one liberally with butter and season them well with salt and ground pepper.

Heat the remaining olive oil in a large saucepan, add the onion, carrot, celery, and remaining garlic, and cook them for 5 minutes. Pour in the red wine, cook for another 5 minutes, then add the beef stock, bay leaves, and the remaining thyme. Mix the cornstarch with 1 tablespoon water until it is smooth and add it to the pan. Simmer the sauce over low heat for 20 minutes or until it is slightly thickened, then strain and season to taste with salt and pepper.

Preheat a covered barbecue to medium indirect heat, put the sirloin in the middle of the barbecue, and arrange the potatoes around it. Replace the cover and cook for 45 minutes.

Remove the sirloin from the barbecue and leave it to rest, covered, for about 10 minutes before carving. Serve the steak with the hasselback potatoes and red wine sauce. Delicious with grilled asparagus (see page 346).

Serves 6–8

# Mirin and sake chicken

4 large chicken breast fillets
2 tablespoons mirin
2 tablespoons sake
1 tablespoon vegetable oil
2-inch piece of fresh ginger, very
  finely sliced
3 teaspoons soy sauce
salad leaves, to serve

Put the chicken in a nonmetallic dish. Combine the mirin, sake, and oil and pour over the chicken. Marinate for 15 minutes, then drain the chicken, reserving the marinade.

Cook the chicken on a hot, lightly oiled barbecue grill or flat plate for 4 minutes each side or until tender.

Put the ginger in a pan and add the reserved marinade. Boil for about 7 minutes or until thickened. Drizzle the soy sauce over the chicken and top with the ginger. Serve immediately on a bed of salad leaves.

Serves 4

# Honey roasted pork fillet

1 tablespoon finely grated fresh
  ginger
6 garlic cloves
1/3 cup soy sauce
2 tablespoons vegetable oil
4 lb. 8 oz. piece pork neck or
  blade roast
2 tablespoons honey

Mix the ginger, garlic, soy sauce, and oil in a large nonmetallic bowl. Put the pork in the marinade and turn it so that it is well coated, then cover the bowl and refrigerate it overnight.

Remove the pork from the marinade, pour the marinade into a small saucepan, and simmer it over low heat for 5 minutes or until it is slightly reduced. Stir the honey into the warm marinade and remove it from the heat. Preheat a covered barbecue to low–medium indirect heat, then put the pork in the middle of the barbecue and roast it, covered, for 45 minutes or until it is cooked through. In the last 10 minutes of cooking, baste the roast all over with the reduced marinade. Be careful not to let any of the marinade splash onto the grill, as it may burn and stick. Remove the roast from the grill and put it on a tray, covered, to cool for 10 minutes.

Carve the roast and serve it with any pan juices left in the tray. Warm parsley carrots (see page 341) make the perfect accompaniment.

Serves 6–8

## Bacon-wrapped chicken

2 tablespoons olive oil
2 tablespoons lime juice
$\frac{1}{4}$ teaspoon ground coriander
6 chicken breast fillets
4 tablespoons fruit chutney
3 tablespoons chopped pecans
6 slices bacon

Mix together the olive oil, lime juice, and coriander and season with salt and pepper. Using a sharp knife, cut a pocket in the thickest section of each fillet. Mix together the chutney and pecans. Spoon 1 tablespoon of the chutney mixture into each chicken breast pocket.

Turn the tapered ends of the fillets to the underside. Wrap a slice of bacon around each fillet to enclose the filling, then secure with a toothpick.

Put the chicken parcels on a hot, lightly oiled barbecue grill or flat plate and cook for 5 minutes on each side or until cooked through, turning once. Brush with the lime juice mixture several times during cooking and drizzle with any leftover lime juice mixture to serve.

Serves 6

Note: This recipe also works well with prosciutto, which is the Italian equivalent of bacon.

## Marinated lamb

½ cup finely chopped Italian parsley
⅓ cup finely chopped cilantro
4 garlic cloves, crushed
1 tablespoon paprika
1 teaspoon dried thyme
½ cup olive oil
¼ cup lemon juice
2 teaspoons ground cumin
4 lamb rumps, 9 oz. each, or pieces
  of tenderloin, trimmed
white pepper, to taste

Mix the parsley, cilantro, garlic, paprika, thyme, oil, lemon juice, and 1½ teaspoons cumin together in a nonmetallic dish. Score diagonal lines in the fat on the lamb pieces with a sharp knife, then put them in the marinade, turning so they are evenly coated. Cover and refrigerate for at least 2 hours or overnight.

Heat a barbecue flat plate to medium heat. Season the lamb with white pepper, the remaining ½ teaspoon of cumin, and some salt. Cook the rumps fat-side up for 3 minutes and then cook the other side for 2–3 minutes, making sure the fat is well cooked. Take the lamb off the barbecue as soon as it is done, cover it with foil, and put it aside to rest for about 5 minutes before carving. This dish is delicious served with Moroccan spiced carrot salad (see page 313).

Serves 4

# Chinese barbecue pork with pancakes

2 tablespoons sugar
2 tablespoons light soy sauce
2 tablespoons hoisin sauce
2 tablespoons dark soy sauce
2 tablespoons rice wine
2 tablespoons yellow bean paste
   (see Notes)
2 teaspoons sesame oil
1 teaspoon five-spice powder
1/4 teaspoon white pepper
2 garlic cloves, crushed
1 teaspoon finely grated fresh ginger
2 lb. 4 oz. pork fillet
1 tablespoon honey
24 Peking duck pancakes (see Notes)
1 cucumber, seeded and cut into
   3 x 1/4-inch strips
4 scallions, cut into 3 x 1/4-inch strips
1/2 cup plum sauce

Put the sugar, light soy sauce, hoisin sauce, dark soy sauce, rice wine, yellow bean paste, sesame oil, five-spice powder, garlic, ginger, and white pepper in a large nonmetallic bowl. Mix them together well, add the pork fillet, and turn it until it is thoroughly coated in the marinade. Cover and refrigerate it for at least 2 hours or preferably overnight.

Take the pork out of the refrigerator and allow it to come back to room temperature. Drain the marinade into a small saucepan, add the honey, and simmer it over low heat for about 5 minutes or until it has reduced slightly. Preheat a barbecue grill to medium direct heat and cook the pork fillet on the grill for 20 minutes or until it is caramelized and cooked through, turning and basting it with the honey marinade mixture in the last 5–8 minutes of cooking. Allow the fillet to cool for 5 minutes before slicing.

Wrap the pancakes in foil and set them on a warm place on the grill while the pork is cooling so that they heat through without cooking or burning. Put the sliced pork and warm pancakes out with the rest of the fillings and let everyone make their own pancake parcels by wrapping some sliced pork,

cucumber, scallions, and plum sauce in their pancake.

Serves 6

Notes: Yellow bean paste is made from fermented yellow soybeans and is available from Asian markets. Frozen Peking duck pancakes are also available from Asian markets.

# Roast beef with barbecue sauce

2 tablespoons paprika
1 tablespoon onion powder
1 tablespoon garlic powder
2 teaspoons sugar
1 teaspoon chili powder
1/4 cup vegetable oil
3 lb. 5 oz. piece beef fillet

*Barbecue sauce*
2 tablespoons vegetable oil
1 small onion, finely chopped
4 garlic cloves, crushed
1/2 teaspoon chili flakes
1 tablespoon paprika
1/2 teaspoon smoked paprika
1 1/2 cups tomato sauce
1/2 cup beer
1/4 cup cider vinegar
1/3 cup brown sugar
2 tablespoons Dijon mustard
1/3 cup Worcestershire sauce

Mix the paprika, onion powder, garlic powder, sugar, chili powder, 2 teaspoons ground black pepper, 2 teaspoons salt, and the oil in a small bowl. Rub the mixture all over the beef fillet, then cover it with plastic wrap and refrigerate overnight.

To make the barbecue sauce, put the oil in a small saucepan over medium heat, add the onion, garlic, and chili flakes, and cook them for 5 minutes or until the onion is soft. Add the remaining ingredients and 1/4 cup water and let the sauce simmer over low heat for 20 minutes or until it is slightly thickened. Season well and let it cool.

Preheat a covered barbecue to medium indirect heat. Put the beef fillet in the middle of the barbecue and cook, covered, for 40 minutes for rare beef. If you would like medium beef, roast for another 10 minutes.

Brush the barbecue sauce all over the beef fillet and cook it, covered, for another 10 minutes. Remove the beef from the barbecue, cover it loosely with foil, and let it cool for 10 minutes before carving and serving it with the remaining barbecue sauce.

Serves 6

# Barbecued tuna and white bean salad

14 oz. tuna steaks
1 small red onion, thinly sliced
1 tomato, seeded and chopped
1 small red pepper, thinly sliced
2 (14-oz.) cans cannellini beans
2 garlic cloves, crushed
1 teaspoon chopped thyme
4 tablespoons finely chopped
  Italian parsley
1½ tablespoons lemon juice
⅓ cup extra-virgin olive oil
1 teaspoon honey
4 handfuls arugula

Place the tuna steaks on a plate, sprinkle with cracked black pepper on both sides, cover with plastic wrap, and refrigerate until needed.

Combine the onion, tomato, and pepper in a large bowl. Rinse the cannellini beans under cold running water for 30 seconds, drain, and add to the bowl with the garlic, thyme, and 3 tablespoons of the parsley.

Place the lemon juice, oil, and honey in a small saucepan, bring to a boil, then simmer, stirring, for 1 minute or until the honey dissolves. Remove from the heat.

Cook the tuna on a hot, lightly oiled barbecue grill or flat plate for 1 minute on each side. The meat should still be pink in the middle. Slice into small cubes and combine with the salad. Toss with the warm dressing.

Arrange the arugula on a platter. Top with the salad, season well, and toss with the remaining parsley.

Serves 4–6

# Blackened Cajun spiced chicken

1 1/2 tablespoons onion powder
1 1/2 tablespoons garlic powder
2 teaspoons paprika
1 teaspoon white pepper
2 teaspoons dried thyme
1/2–1 teaspoon chili powder
8 chicken drumsticks, scored

Combine the onion powder, garlic powder, paprika, white pepper, thyme, chili powder, and 1 teaspoon salt in a plastic bag. Place the drumsticks in the bag and shake until all the pieces are coated. Leave the chicken in the refrigerator for at least 30 minutes or overnight to allow the flavors to develop.

Cook the chicken on a lightly oiled barbecue grill for 55–60 minutes or until slightly blackened and cooked through. Brush lightly with some oil to keep it from drying out while cooking.

Serves 4

# Fillet steak with flavored butters

4 fillet steaks

*Red pepper butter*
1 small red pepper
1/2 cup butter
2 teaspoons chopped oregano
2 teaspoons chopped chives

*Garlic butter*
1/2 cup butter
3 garlic cloves, crushed
2 scallions, finely chopped

Cut a pocket in each steak.

For the red pepper butter, cut the pepper into large pieces and place them skin-side up on a hot grill until the skin blisters and blackens. Put in a plastic bag until cool, then peel away the skin and dice the flesh. Beat the butter until creamy. Add the pepper, oregano, and chives, season, and beat until smooth.

For the garlic butter, beat the butter until creamy, add the garlic and scallions, and beat until smooth.

Push red pepper butter into the pockets in two of the steaks and garlic butter into the other two. Cook on a hot, lightly oiled barbecue grill or flat plate for 4–5 minutes each side, turning once. Brush frequently with any remaining flavored butter while cooking. These steaks are delicious served with a simple green salad.

Serves 4

# Roast rack of pork with chunky applesauce and vegetables

6 Granny Smith apples
⅓ cup sugar
¼ cup white wine vinegar
2 tablespoons finely shredded
   mint leaves
1 rack of pork with 6 ribs
   (about 3 lb. 8 oz.)
1 tablespoon olive oil

*Roasted vegetables*
2 orange sweet potatoes
2 lb. 4 oz. squash
12 small onions
6 carrots
⅓ cup olive oil
6 garlic cloves, unpeeled
2 tablespoons finely chopped
   Italian parsley

Peel the apples, remove the seeds, and roughly dice the flesh. Simmer them over low heat with the sugar, vinegar, and 1/4 cup water in a small saucepan for 15 minutes or until they are cooked through and just beginning to collapse. Remove the sauce from the heat and stir in the shredded mint.

Score the skin on the rack of pork in a large diamond pattern, rub the oil all over the pork, then rub 1 teaspoon salt into the skin. To make the roast vegetables, peel the sweet potatoes, squash, onions, and carrots and cut them into large, even pieces. Toss the vegetables with 2 tablespoons of olive oil until they are coated, then season them well with salt and freshly ground black pepper. Trim the root end from the garlic cloves, drizzle 1/2 teaspoon of oil over them, and wrap them in a double layer of foil.

Preheat a covered barbecue to medium indirect heat. Put the pork rack in the middle of the barbecue, cover it, and roast for about 1 hour 20 minutes or until the juices run clear when a skewer is inserted into the thickest part of the flesh. When the pork has been cooking for about 20 minutes, arrange the vegetables around the roast and cook them, covered, for 1 hour or until they are golden and tender. Add the garlic to the barbecue and cook it for 30 minutes or until it has softened.

When the garlic cloves are cool enough to handle, squeeze them from their skin, mash them with the remaining olive oil, and stir in the chopped parsley. Season with salt and ground pepper and drizzle the dressing over the roast vegetables just before serving.

When the pork is cooked, remove it from the barbecue and leave it to cool, covered, for 10 minutes. Slice between the bones and serve it with the roasted vegetables and chunky applesauce.

Serves 6

# Honey mustard chicken

½ cup honey
¼ cup Dijon mustard
2 tablespoons vegetable oil
2 tablespoons white wine vinegar
3 garlic cloves, crushed
2 tablespoons chopped parsley
   leaves
4-lb. whole chicken, cut into
   10 pieces

Put the honey, mustard, oil, white wine vinegar, garlic, parsley, and ¼ teaspoon freshly ground black pepper in a large nonmetallic bowl. Mix it all together well and put aside ¼ cup of the marinade to baste the chicken during cooking. Add the chicken pieces to the rest of the marinade and turn them so that they are thoroughly coated. Cover the bowl and refrigerate it for at least 4 hours or overnight.

Preheat a covered barbecue to medium indirect heat and cook the chicken pieces for 20–30 minutes or until they are cooked through. The breast pieces may take as little as 15 minutes, while dark meat will take longer. Baste the chicken with the reserved marinade during the last 5–8 minutes of cooking, but no earlier or it could burn. This is delicious served on a bed of mashed potatoes with scallions (see page 310).

Serves 4–6

# Stuffed baby calamari with lime and chili dipping sauce

*Dipping sauce*
1/3 cup lime juice
1/4 cup fish sauce
2 tablespoons brown sugar
1 small red chili, finely sliced
  into rounds

12 medium baby calamari
12 raw shrimp, peeled, deveined,
  and chopped
5 1/2 oz. ground pork
4 garlic cloves, crushed
1/2 teaspoon finely grated fresh
  ginger
3 teaspoons fish sauce
2 teaspoons lime juice
1 teaspoon brown sugar
2 tablespoons chopped cilantro
peanut oil, for brushing

For the dipping sauce, put the lime juice, fish sauce, brown sugar, and chili in a bowl and stir it together until the sugar has dissolved. Cover.

Gently pull the tentacles away from the calamari tubes (the intestines should come away at the same time). Remove the quill from inside the body and discard, as well as any white membrane. Pull the skin away from the hood under running water, then cut the tentacles away from the intestines and rinse them to remove the sucker rings. Finely chop the tentacles to add to the stuffing.

Put the shrimp, pork, garlic, ginger, fish sauce, juice, sugar, cilantro, and chopped tentacles in a bowl and mix together. Use a spoon to put the stuffing in each tube and push it to the bottom, then secure the hole with a toothpick. Don't overfill the tubes, as the stuffing will expand when cooked.

Preheat the grill to medium, brush the squid tubes with peanut oil, and cook them for 8 minutes or until cooked, turning when the flesh becomes opaque and slightly charred. Remove the toothpicks and cut each tube into thin rounds. Serve with the dipping sauce.

Serves 4

## Fennel and pork sausages with onion relish

1 lb. 10 oz. ground pork
1/2 cup fresh bread crumbs
2 garlic cloves, crushed
3 teaspoons fennel seeds, coarsely crushed
1 teaspoon finely grated orange zest
2 teaspoons chopped thyme leaves
1/4 cup chopped Italian parsley
vegetable oil, for brushing
1 long baguette, cut into 4 pieces, or 4 long, crusty rolls
4 tablespoons butter, softened
2 1/4 oz. arugula
1 tablespoon extra-virgin olive oil
1 teaspoon balsamic vinegar

*Onion relish*
4 tablespoons butter
2 red onions, thinly sliced
1 tablespoon brown sugar
2 tablespoons balsamic vinegar

Put the pork, bread crumbs, garlic, fennel seeds, zest, thyme, and parsley in a large bowl, season well with salt and freshly ground black pepper, and mix it all together with your hands. Cover the mixture and refrigerate it for 4 hours or overnight.

To make the onion relish, melt the butter in a heavy-based saucepan, add the onion, and cook, stirring occasionally, over low heat for about 10 minutes or until the onion is softened but not browned. Add the sugar and vinegar and continue to cook for another 30 minutes, stirring regularly.

Preheat a barbecue flat plate to medium heat. Divide the pork mixture into eight portions and use wet hands to mold each portion into a flat sausage shape. Lightly brush the sausages with oil and cook them for 8 minutes on each side or until they are cooked through.

To assemble, split the rolls down the middle and butter them. Toss the arugula with the olive oil and balsamic vinegar and put some of the leaves in each of the rolls. Top with a sausage and some of the onion relish.

Makes 8

# Rosemary lamb on grilled polenta with anchovy sauce

1 lb. 5 oz. lamb fillets
1 tablespoon finely chopped
  rosemary leaves
3 garlic cloves, bruised
2 tablespoons olive oil
1 tablespoon lemon juice
1²/₃ cups instant polenta
1/3 cup grated Parmesan cheese
1 tablespoon butter
1¹/₂ cups arugula leaves

*Anchovy and rosemary sauce*
8 large anchovy fillets, chopped
3 teaspoons finely chopped
  rosemary leaves
³/₄ cup olive oil
1 tablespoon lemon juice

Trim the lamb fillets of any fat and sinew and put them in a nonmetallic bowl with the rosemary, garlic, olive oil, and lemon juice, turning the fillets until they are well coated. Season with pepper, cover the bowl, and refrigerate it for at least 4 hours or preferably overnight.

Meanwhile, to make the polenta, bring 4 cups of salted water to a boil in a heavy-based saucepan. Whisking constantly, add the polenta in a thin stream and stir until it thickens and starts to come away from the side of the pan. Remove the pan from the heat and add the Parmesan and butter, then season generously with salt and freshly ground black pepper. Stir the polenta until the cheese and butter have melted, then pour it into a lightly greased, 9-inch square baking pan and smooth the surface. Refrigerate the polenta for 2 hours or until it is cool and firm, then turn it out onto a chopping board, trim the edges, and cut the block into four squares.

While the polenta is cooling, make the anchovy and rosemary sauce. Put the anchovies and rosemary in a food processor and blend them to a paste. Add the olive oil in a thin stream, then add the lemon juice and season with salt and pepper.

Preheat a barbecue grill to medium heat. Grill the polenta squares for 7–8 minutes on each side or until they are crisp and golden. When the polenta is ready, move the squares to the side of the grill, season the lamb fillets with salt, and cook for 2–3 minutes each side for medium–rare or until cooked to your liking.

To serve, slice the lamb fillets diagonally into four pieces, cutting across the grain. Put the grilled polenta on warmed serving plates, top it with the lamb and arugula, and drizzle with the sauce.

Serves 4

## Lemon and sage marinated veal chops with arugula

4 veal chops
2 tablespoons olive oil
1 tablespoon lemon juice
4 strips lemon zest
1/4 cup roughly chopped sage leaves
3 garlic cloves, peeled and bruised
lemon wedges, to serve

*Arugula salad*
3 1/2 oz. arugula, washed and picked
1 avocado, sliced
1 1/2 tablespoons extra-virgin olive oil
2 teaspoons balsamic vinegar

Trim any fat and sinew from the chops and put them in a shallow nonmetallic dish with the olive oil, lemon juice, lemon zest, sage, and garlic. Turn the chops so that they are evenly coated, then season them with freshly ground black pepper, cover, and refrigerate for 4 hours or preferably overnight.

Put the arugula in a large serving bowl and sprinkle the avocado on top. Drizzle the olive oil and balsamic vinegar over the salad, season it with a little salt and ground black pepper, and toss gently.

Preheat a barbecue grill to medium–high heat. Remove the chops from the marinade, season well with salt, and grill them for 5–6 minutes on each side or until cooked to your liking. Remove the chops from the barbecue, cover them loosely with foil, and let them cool for 5 minutes.

Put the chops on a serving plate, drizzle with any juices that have been released while they cooled, and serve with the arugula salad and lemon wedges.

Serves 4

## Chinese-style barbecue spareribs

¼ cup hoisin sauce
⅓ cup oyster sauce
2 tablespoons rice wine
½ cup soy sauce
6 garlic cloves, crushed
1 tablespoon finely grated fresh ginger
4 lb. 8 oz. pork spareribs
2 tablespoons honey

Mix the hoisin sauce, oyster sauce, rice wine, soy sauce, garlic, and ginger in a large nonmetallic bowl, add the ribs, and turn them so that they are coated in the marinade. Cover the bowl and refrigerate for at least 4 hours or overnight.

Remove the ribs from the marinade and tip the marinade into a small saucepan with the honey. Simmer the mixture over low heat for 5 minutes or until it becomes slightly syrupy—you will be using this to baste the ribs as they cook.

Heat a covered barbecue to medium indirect heat and cook the ribs, covered, for 10 minutes, then turn them over and cook them for another 5 minutes. Continue cooking, basting and turning the ribs frequently, for 30 minutes or until they are cooked through and caramelized all over.

Once the ribs are cooked, let them cool, covered, for 10 minutes, then cut the racks into individual ribs to serve. Make sure there are plenty of napkins available—these ribs should be eaten with your fingers and are deliciously sticky.

Serves 6

## Teriyaki baby octopus

½ cup sake
½ cup mirin
½ cup dark soy sauce
1 tablespoon superfine sugar
2 teaspoons grated fresh ginger
2 garlic cloves, finely chopped
2 lb. 4 oz. baby octopus

Combine the sake, mirin, dark soy sauce, and sugar in a small saucepan. Bring the mixture to a boil over medium heat and cook, stirring until all the sugar has dissolved, then add the ginger and garlic and remove the saucepan from the heat. Leave the mixture to cool for 30 minutes.

To prepare the octopus, use a small knife to carefully cut between the head and tentacles of the octopus, just below the eyes. Push the beak out and up through the tentacles with your finger, then remove the eyes from the head of the octopus by cutting off a small disk and discarding it. To clean the octopus tube, carefully slit through one side, avoiding the ink sac, and scrape out any gut. Rinse the inside under running water to remove any remaining gut and cut it in half. Wash the rest of the octopus thoroughly under running water, pulling the skin away from the tube and tentacles. If the tentacles are large, cut them into quarters.

Put the octopus in a large nonmetallic bowl. Whisk the teriyaki marinade, making sure that it is well combined, then pour it over the octopus, stirring so that the octopus is thoroughly coated. Cover and marinate it in the refrigerator for at least 2 hours or overnight.

Preheat a barbecue grill to medium heat. Remove the octopuses from the teriyaki marinade and cook for 2–3 minutes or until they are cooked through, curled, and glazed. Delicious served on a bed of Asian salad (see page 345).

Serves 4

# Sides

## Pear and walnut salad

¼ cup walnut oil
1¼ tablespoons sherry vinegar
1 teaspoon Dijon mustard
3 ripe pears, halved, cored, and cut
  into ½-inch-thick wedges
4 tablespoons butter, melted
1 tablespoon brown sugar
2 heads Belgian endive, leaves
  separated
⅔ cup walnut pieces, toasted and
  chopped

To make the salad dressing, whisk the walnut oil, vinegar, mustard, and some freshly ground black pepper in a bowl. Put the pears, melted butter, and sugar in a bowl and toss them together until the pears are well coated in the butter.

Cook the pear slices on a barbecue flat plate preheated to medium–high for 1 minute each side or until they are golden and slightly caramelized, basting with the butter and sugar mixture during cooking.

Put the endive in a large bowl, add the dressing, walnuts, and pears, toss well, and serve.

Serves 4

## Grilled mangoes

3 small mangoes
2 teaspoons vegetable oil

Preheat a barbecue to medium. To prepare the mangoes, cut each cheek straight down on either side of the pit. Score the flesh without cutting through the skin and lightly brush the cut surface with the oil.

Cook the mangoes on the grill, skin-side down, for 2 minutes, then turn them 90 degrees and cook for another 2 minutes to make crossed grill marks. Serve warm.

Serves 4–6

# Eggplant, tomato, and sumac salad

2 eggplants, cut into ½-inch-thick
  rounds
½ cup olive oil
5 large ripe tomatoes
1 small red onion, finely sliced
⅓ cup roughly chopped mint leaves
⅓ cup roughly chopped Italian parsley
2 teaspoons sumac (see Note)
2 tablespoons lemon juice

Put the eggplant slices in a colander and sprinkle them with salt. Leave the eggplant for 30 minutes to allow some of the bitter juices to drain away, then rinse the slices and pat them dry with paper towels. Using 2 tablespoons of the olive oil, brush both sides of each slice, then grill them for 5 minutes on each side or until they are cooked through. Let the slices cool slightly, then cut them in half.

Cut the tomatoes into wedges and arrange them in a serving bowl with the eggplant and onion. Sprinkle the mint, parsley, and sumac over the top, then put the lemon juice and remaining olive oil in a small screw-top jar, season, and shake it up. Drizzle the dressing over the salad and toss it gently.

Serves 6

Note: Sumac is a spice made from crushing the dried sumac berry. It has a mild lemony flavor and is used extensively in many cuisines, from North Africa and the Middle East to India and Asia.

# Grilled potatoes with pistachio salsa

*Pistachio salsa*
1 cup pistachio nuts, toasted
2 ripe tomatoes, chopped
2 garlic cloves, finely chopped
1 small red chili, finely chopped
2 tablespoons chopped Italian parsley
1 tablespoon chopped mint
1 teaspoon finely grated lemon zest

1 lb. 10 oz. (about 5 medium)
   potatoes
3 tablespoons all-purpose flour
2 tablespoons olive oil
sour cream, to serve

To make the pistachio salsa, roughly chop the nuts and combine with the tomato, garlic, chili, herbs, and lemon zest. Season with salt and pepper.

Peel the potatoes and cut into large wedges. Place in a pan and cover with water, bring to a boil, and cook for 5 minutes. Transfer to a colander and rinse under running water to stop the cooking. Pat the wedges dry with paper towels.

Sprinkle the flour over the potatoes in a bowl and toss to lightly coat. Cook the potato wedges in a single layer on a hot, lightly oiled barbecue flat plate or grill for 5–10 minutes or until golden brown and tender. Drizzle with the olive oil and turn the potatoes regularly during cooking. Serve with the salsa and a bowl of sour cream.

Serves 4

# Tabbouleh

3/4 cup bulgur wheat
3 ripe tomatoes
1 large cucumber
1/3 cup lemon juice
1/4 cup olive oil
1 tablespoon extra-virgin olive oil
4 scallions, sliced
4 cups chopped Italian parsley
1/4 oz. chopped mint

Place the bulgur in a bowl, cover with 2 cups water, and leave it for 1 1/2 hours. Cut the tomatoes in half, squeeze the halves gently to remove any excess seeds, and cut the flesh into 1/4-inch cubes. Cut the cucumber in half lengthwise, remove the seeds, and cut the flesh into 1/4-inch cubes. Drain the bulgur, squeezing out any excess water, and spread it out across a clean towel for 30 minutes to dry.

Whisk together the lemon juice and 1 1/2 teaspoons of salt until they are well combined. Season the dressing with pepper, then slowly whisk in the olive oil and extra-virgin olive oil. Put the bulgur in a large bowl and add the tomato, cucumber, scallions, parsley, and mint. Toss the dressing with the tabbouleh, then cover and refrigerate.

Serves 4–6

# Smoky tomato sauce

*Smoking mix*
2 tablespoons Chinese or Ceylon
   tea leaves
2 star anise, crushed
1 strip orange zest
1/2 teaspoon five-spice powder
6 juniper berries, crushed

2 onions, quartered
2 red peppers, cut into large pieces
2 red chilies, cut in half
3 tablespoons vegetable oil
3 garlic cloves, chopped
3 medium tomatoes, chopped
2 tablespoons Worcestershire sauce
1/2 cup barbecue sauce
2 tablespoons tamarind concentrate
1 tablespoon white wine vinegar
1 tablespoon brown sugar

Combine all the ingredients for the smoking mix in a bowl. Pour the mix into the center of a sheet of foil and fold the edges to prevent spreading. (This will form an open container to allow the mix to smoke.) Place the foil container on the bottom of a dry wok or wide frying pan. Put an open rack or steamer in the wok or frying pan, making sure it is elevated over the mix.

Place the onion, pepper, and chili on the rack and cover with a lid or, alternatively, cover the entire wok or frying pan tightly with foil to prevent the smoke from escaping.

Smoke over medium heat for about 10–15 minutes or until the vegetables are tender. For a very smoky sauce, cook the vegetables for longer; if you prefer it less smoky, reduce the time. Remove the smoking mix container.

Dice the onion, pepper, and chili very finely. Heat the oil in the wok and add the garlic and cooked vegetables. Fry over medium heat for 3 minutes, then add the tomato and cook until pulpy. Add the sauces, tamarind, vinegar, and sugar. Simmer, stirring occasionally, for about 20–25 minutes or until the sauce is quite thick. Store in the refrigerator.

Makes about 4 cups sauce

## Fennel salad

2 large fennel bulbs
1 tablespoon lemon juice
1 tablespoon extra-virgin olive oil
2 teaspoons red wine vinegar
1/2 cup Niçoise olives, pitted

Trim the fennel bulbs, reserving the fronds, and discard the tough outer layers. Using a very sharp knife, slice the fennel lengthwise as thinly as possible and put it in a bowl of very cold water with the lemon juice.

Just before you are ready to serve the main meal, drain the fennel well, pat it dry with paper towels, and toss it in a bowl with the olive oil and red wine vinegar. Finely chop the fennel fronds, add them to the fennel with the olives, and season to taste with freshly ground black pepper.

Serves 4

# Mashed potatoes with scallions

2 lb. 4 oz. (about 6 medium) floury
  potatoes (such as russet)
2 tablespoons butter
⅓ cup milk
¼ cup cream
3 scallions, finely sliced

Peel the potatoes and cut them into large chunks. Steam or boil the pieces for 12 minutes or until they are tender, then drain the water away and briefly return the potatoes to the heat, shaking the pan, to remove any excess moisture.

Add the butter, milk, and cream and mash the potatoes until they are smooth. Stir in the scallions, season to taste, and serve warm.

Serves 4–6

## Moroccan spiced carrot salad

4 carrots, peeled, trimmed, and
  halved diagonally
1/3 cup olive oil
2 teaspoons ground cumin
1/2 cup kalamata olives, pitted and
  halved lengthwise
1/4 cup Italian parsley
1/2–1 teaspoon harissa
2 tablespoons extra-virgin olive oil
1 tablespoon red wine vinegar

Bring a saucepan of salted water to a boil and blanch the carrots for 3 minutes or until they just begin to soften. Drain well, pat dry with paper towels, then toss them with 2 tablespoons of the olive oil and 1 teaspoon of the cumin. Cook the carrots on a hot griddle or barbecue plate for 25 minutes, turning them once, until they are cooked through and golden all over.

While the carrots are still warm, cut them into thin diagonal slices and toss them with the olives and parsley. Mix the harissa with 1 tablespoon of water, add the extra-virgin olive oil, red wine vinegar, and the remaining olive oil and cumin, and whisk it together. Pour the dressing over the salad and season to taste with salt and pepper. Serve warm.

Serves 4

# Barbecued corn on the cob

8 fresh ears of corn
1/2 cup olive oil
6 garlic cloves, chopped
4 tablespoons chopped Italian parsley
butter, to serve

Peel back the corn husks, leaving them intact. Pull off the white silks, then wash the corn and pat dry with paper towels.

Combine the olive oil, garlic, parsley, and some salt and black pepper and brush over each cob. Pull up the husks and tie together at the top with string. Steam over boiling water for 5 minutes, then pat dry.

Cook on a hot, lightly oiled barbecue grill or flat plate for 20 minutes, turning regularly. Spray with water during the cooking to keep the corn moist. Serve hot with knobs of butter.

Serves 8

## Asian rice salad

2 cups long-grain rice
2 tablespoons olive oil
1 large red onion, finely chopped
4 garlic cloves, crushed
1 tablespoon finely chopped fresh
   ginger
1 long red chili, seeded and thinly
   sliced
4 scallions, finely sliced
2 tablespoons soy sauce
1/2 teaspoon sesame oil
2 teaspoons black vinegar
   (see Note)
1 tablespoon lime juice
1 cup roughly chopped cilantro

Bring 5 cups of water to a boil in a large saucepan. Add the rice and cook it, uncovered, for 12–15 minutes over low heat or until the grains are tender. Drain and rinse the rice under cold running water, then transfer it to a large bowl.

While the rice is cooking, heat the oil in a frying pan over medium heat. Add the onion, garlic, ginger, and chili and cook them for 5–6 minutes or until the onion has softened but not browned. Stir in the scallions and cook for another minute. Remove the onion mixture from the heat and add it to the rice with the soy sauce, sesame oil, vinegar, lime juice, and cilantro and mix well. Cover the rice salad and refrigerate until you are ready to serve.

Serves 4

Note: Black vinegar is a type of Chinese vinegar and can be found in Asian markets.

## Pineapple mint salsa

1 small ripe pineapple
1 tablespoon brown sugar
1 small red chili, seeded and finely
  diced
1/2 teaspoon rice vinegar
2 tablespoons lime juice
4 scallions, finely chopped
1/4 cup chopped mint leaves

Peel the pineapple, remove all of the "eyes," and slice it lengthwise into quarters. Remove the central core and cut the flesh into 1/2-inch dice. Put the pineapple in a nonmetallic mixing bowl with the sugar, chili, rice vinegar, lime juice, scallions, and mint and stir them together. Cover the bowl and refrigerate for 1 hour to let the flavors develop.

Serves 4

# Red pepper relish

2 lb. 4 oz. red peppers
1 teaspoon black peppercorns
2 teaspoons black mustard seeds
2 red onions, thinly sliced
4 garlic cloves, chopped
1½ cups red wine vinegar
2 apples, peeled, cored, and grated
1 teaspoon grated fresh ginger
1 cup brown sugar

Remove the pepper seeds and membrane and slice thinly. Tie the peppercorns in a piece of muslin and secure with string. Combine the peppers, peppercorns, mustard seeds, onion, garlic, vinegar, apples, and ginger in a large pan. Simmer, covered, for 30 minutes or until the pepper is soft.

Add the sugar and stir over low heat until completely dissolved. Cover and simmer, stirring occasionally, for 1¼ hours or until the relish has reduced and thickened. Remove the muslin bag.

Rinse the jars with boiling water, then dry in a warm oven. Spoon the relish into the hot jars and seal. Turn the jars upside down for 2 minutes, then turn them the other way up and leave to cool. Label and date. Leave for a few weeks before using. Will keep in a cool, dark place for 1 year. Refrigerate after opening.

Fills three 8-oz. jars

## Avocado and grapefruit salad

2 ruby grapefruit
1 ripe avocado
7 oz. watercress leaves
1 French shallot, finely sliced
1 tablespoon sherry vinegar
1/4 cup olive oil

Peel and segment the grapefruit, working over a bowl to save any juice for the dressing. Cut the avocado into 3/4-inch wedges and put in a bowl with the watercress, grapefruit, and shallot.

Put 1 tablespoon of the reserved grapefruit juice in a small screw-top jar with the sherry vinegar, olive oil, salt, and black pepper, and shake it up. Pour the dressing over the salad and toss gently.

Serves 4

# Grilled cauliflower salad with tahini dressing and gremolata

*Tahini dressing*
1/4 cup tahini
1 garlic clove, crushed
1/4 cup rice vinegar
1 tablespoon vegetable oil
1/4 teaspoon sesame oil
1 teaspoon lemon juice

2 teaspoons sesame seeds, toasted
1 tablespoon finely chopped Italian parsley
1/2 small garlic clove, finely chopped
1/2 teaspoon finely grated lemon zest
1 cauliflower (about 4 lb.)
2 tablespoons vegetable oil
2 heads romaine lettuce, washed and drained
1 3/4 oz. watercress leaves, washed and drained

To make the dressing, whisk the tahini, garlic, rice vinegar, oils, lemon juice, and 1 tablespoon of water together and season to taste. Stir the sesame seeds, parsley, garlic, and lemon zest together.

Divide the cauliflower into large florets and cut each floret into 1/2-inch-thick slices. Brush the slices with oil and season well. Preheat a barbecue grill to medium heat and grill the cauliflower pieces for 6–8 minutes or until they are cooked and golden on both sides.

Arrange the lettuce leaves and watercress on a serving plate and top them with the grilled cauliflower slices. Drizzle the tahini dressing over the cauliflower, sprinkle with the sesame seed mixture, and serve it while it is still hot.

Serves 4

# Minted potato salad

1 lb. 5 oz. new potatoes, large
  ones halved
½ cup thick plain yogurt
1 small cucumber, grated and
  squeezed dry
¼ cup finely chopped mint leaves
2 garlic cloves, crushed

Boil or steam the potatoes for
10 minutes or until they are tender,
then leave them to cool. Mix together
the yogurt, cucumber, mint, and
garlic and toss it through the cooled
potatoes. Season well and serve.

Serves 4

## Barbecue sauce

2 teaspoons vegetable oil
1 small onion, finely chopped
1 tablespoon malt vinegar
1 tablespoon brown sugar
1/3 cup tomato sauce
1 tablespoon Worcestershire sauce

Heat the oil in a small pan and cook the onion over low heat for 3 minutes or until soft, stirring occasionally.

Add the remaining ingredients and bring to a boil. Reduce the heat and simmer for 3 minutes, stirring occasionally. Serve warm or at room temperature. Can be kept for up to a week if covered and refrigerated.

Serves 4

# Dill coleslaw

⅓ cup sour cream
2 teaspoons prepared horseradish
1 tablespoon lemon juice
1 tablespoon Dijon mustard
2 tablespoons finely chopped dill
4 cups shredded red cabbage
2 carrots, peeled and grated

Put the sour cream, horseradish, lemon juice, mustard, and dill in a large bowl and stir it together. Add the cabbage and carrots, toss them together well so that the coleslaw is lightly coated with dressing, and season to taste. Cover and refrigerate until ready to serve.

Serves 6–8

# Warm marinated mushroom salad

1 lb. 10 oz. (about 6 cups) mixed
    mushrooms (such as baby button,
    oyster, portobello, shiitake, and
    enoki)
2 garlic cloves, finely chopped
1/2 teaspoon green peppercorns,
    crushed
1/3 cup olive oil
1/3 cup orange juice
9 oz. salad leaves, watercress, or
    baby spinach leaves
1 teaspoon finely grated orange zest

Trim the mushroom stems and wipe the mushrooms with a damp paper towel. Cut any large mushrooms in half. Mix together the garlic, peppercorns, olive oil, and orange juice. Pour over the mushrooms and marinate for about 20 minutes.

Arrange the salad leaves in a large serving dish.

Drain the mushrooms, reserving the marinade. Cook the flat and button mushrooms on a hot, lightly oiled barbecue grill or flat plate for about 2 minutes. Add the softer mushrooms and cook for 1 minute or until they just soften.

Sprinkle the mushrooms over the salad leaves and drizzle with the marinade. Sprinkle with orange zest and season well with salt and pepper.

Serves 4

## Guacamole

2 ripe avocados, mashed
2½ tablespoons lime juice
3 scallions, finely sliced
¼ cup chopped cilantro
1 teaspoon finely chopped red chili

Combine the avocado, lime juice, scallions, cilantro, and chili and season the mixture to taste. Cover the guacamole with plastic wrap, resting the plastic directly on the surface of the mixture, and refrigerate until ready to serve.

Serves 4–6

# Chickpea salad

2 (15-oz.) cans chickpeas (see Note)
3 tomatoes
1 red onion, thinly sliced
1 small red pepper, cut into thin strips
4 scallions, cut into thin strips
1 cup chopped Italian parsley
2–3 tablespoons chopped mint
  leaves

*Dressing*
2 tablespoons tahini
2 tablespoons lemon juice
3 tablespoons olive oil
2 garlic cloves, crushed
1/2 teaspoon ground cumin

Drain the chickpeas and rinse well. Cut the tomatoes in half and remove the seeds with a spoon. Dice the flesh. Mix the red onion, tomato, pepper, and scallions in a bowl. Add the chickpeas, parsley, and mint.

To make the dressing, put all the ingredients in a screw-top jar with 2 tablespoons water, season well, and shake vigorously to make a creamy liquid. Pour over the salad and toss.

Serves 8

Note: If you prefer, you can use dried chickpeas, but they will need to be soaked and cooked first. Use 1 3/4 cups dried chickpeas and put in a pan with 14 cups water and 3 tablespoons olive oil. Partially cover and boil for 2 1/2 hours or until tender. Rinse, drain well, and allow to cool a little before making the salad.

# Baby spinach salad

2 tablespoons olive oil
1 tablespoon lemon juice
5½ oz. baby spinach leaves
½ cup small black olives
sea salt

Whisk together the olive oil and the lemon juice.

Toss the spinach in a large serving bowl with the olives and the combined olive oil and lemon juice. Season the salad with sea salt and freshly ground black pepper.

Serves 4

# Parsley carrots

3 cups baby carrots
2 teaspoons olive oil
2 tablespoons butter
2 tablespoons finely chopped
  Italian parsley

Bring a saucepan of salted water to a boil and blanch the carrots for 3 minutes or until they start to soften. Drain and rinse them under cold water and pat them dry with paper towels. Toss the carrots in olive oil and season with salt and pepper.

When you are nearly ready to serve the main meal, preheat a barbecue grill to medium and cook the carrots for 5 minutes or until they are charred and golden all over. Toss the carrots with the butter and parsley until they are well coated, season to taste with salt and freshly ground black pepper, and serve.

Serves 6–8

## Tomato salsa

4 ripe tomatoes, finely diced
1/4 cup finely chopped red onion
1/2 cup chopped cilantro
1 tablespoon lime juice

Combine the tomato, onion, cilantro, and lime juice, season to taste, then cover the salsa with plastic wrap and refrigerate. Remove the salsa from the refrigerator 15 minutes before you are ready to use it so the ingredients have time to return to room temperature and their full flavor.

Serves 4

## Asian salad

2 sheets nori, cut into 1¼ x ¼-inch
   pieces
2 tablespoons seasoned rice wine
   vinegar
2 teaspoons lemon juice
¼ teaspoon sesame oil
2 teaspoons canola oil
2¼ oz. mizuna leaves
½ cup snow pea shoots
2 small cucumbers, shaved
½ daikon radish, shaved

Toast the nori on a preheated
barbecue plate for 5 minutes to
make it crispy.

To make the dressing, whisk together
the vinegar, lemon juice, sesame oil,
and canola oil. Toss the mizuna, snow
pea shoots, cucumber, daikon radish,
and nori with the dressing and serve.

Serves 4

## Grilled asparagus

1 lb. 2 oz. asparagus
2 garlic cloves, crushed
2 tablespoons balsamic vinegar
2 tablespoons olive oil
2 tablespoons shaved Parmesan
   cheese

Break off the woody ends from the
asparagus by gently bending the
stems until the tough end snaps
away. Cook the asparagus on a hot,
lightly oiled barbecue grill or flat plate
for 3 minutes or until bright green and
just tender.

To make the dressing, whisk the
garlic, vinegar, and olive oil. Pour the
dressing over the warm asparagus
and top with the Parmesan shavings
and lots of black pepper.

Serves 4

## Barbecued baby potatoes

1 lb. 10 oz. baby potatoes, unpeeled
2 tablespoons olive oil
2 tablespoons thyme leaves
2 teaspoons crushed sea salt

Cut any large potatoes in half so that they are all the same size for even cooking. Boil, steam, or microwave the potatoes until just tender. Drain and lightly dry with paper towels.

Put the potatoes in a large bowl and add the oil and thyme. Toss gently and leave for 1 hour.

Lightly oil a barbecue flat plate and preheat it to high heat. Cook the potatoes for 15 minutes, turning frequently and brushing with the remaining oil and thyme mixture, until golden brown. Sprinkle with salt to serve.

Serves 6

Note: The potatoes can be left in the marinade for up to 2 hours before barbecuing, but should be served as soon as they are cooked.

## Cucumber salad

1 long, thin cucumber
1 tablespoon sugar
$1/4$ cup lime juice
1 tablespoon fish sauce
1 red Asian shallot, finely sliced
$1/3$ cup cilantro leaves
1 small red chili, seeds removed,
    finely chopped
$1/2$ cup snow pea shoots

Peel the cucumber, cut it in half lengthwise, remove the seeds, and cut it into $1/4$-inch slices. Put the sugar and lime juice in a large bowl and stir them together until the sugar has dissolved, then add the fish sauce.

Toss the cucumber, shallot, cilantro, and chili through the dressing, then cover and refrigerate for 15 minutes. Just before serving, cut the snow pea shoots in half and stir them through the salad.

Serves 4

# Ratatouille

1 garlic bulb
1/3 cup olive oil
6 Roma tomatoes, halved
   lengthwise
4 baby eggplants, cut diagonally
   into 1/2-inch pieces
3 zucchini, cut diagonally into
   1/2-inch pieces
2 red peppers, seeded and
   cut into wedges
2 red onions, cut into 1/2-inch-thick
   rounds
2 tablespoons balsamic vinegar

Trim the top of the garlic bulb so that the cloves are just exposed, drizzle 1 teaspoon of olive oil over the cut end, and wrap the bulb in foil. Put the garlic on a barbecue that has been preheated to medium indirect heat and cook for 30 minutes or until it has softened.

Lightly brush the vegetables with 2 tablespoons of olive oil and add them to the barbecue when the garlic has been cooking for about 15 minutes. Cook the vegetables for 5–8 minutes on each side or until they are marked and cooked through, then put them in a large bowl.

Squeeze the garlic cloves out of their skins and add to the vegetables. Mix the balsamic vinegar and remaining olive oil together, gently toss it with the ratatouille, and season well.

Serves 6

# Damper

3 cups self-rising flour
1–2 teaspoons salt
6½ tablespoons butter, melted
½ cup milk
milk, extra, to glaze
flour, extra, to dust

Preheat the oven to 415°F. Grease a baking tray. Sift the flour and salt into a bowl and make a well. Combine the butter, milk, and ½ cup water and pour into the well. Stir with a knife until just combined. Turn the dough onto a lightly floured surface and knead for 20 seconds or until smooth. Place the dough on the baking tray and press out to a 6-inch circle.

Using a sharp-pointed knife, score the dough into six sections about ½ inch deep. Brush with milk, then dust with flour. Bake for 10 minutes.

Reduce the oven temperature to 350°F and bake the damper for another 15 minutes or until the damper is golden and sounds hollow when the surface is tapped. Serve with butter.

Makes 1 damper

Note: Damper is the Australian version of soda bread, and is traditionally served warm with slatherings of golden syrup (dark corn syrup). If you prefer, you can make four rounds instead of one large damper and slightly reduce the cooking time. Cut two slashes in the form of a cross on the top.

# Corn bread

1 cup self-rising flour
1 cup fine cornmeal
1 teaspoon salt
1 egg
1 cup buttermilk
¼ cup vegetable oil

Preheat the oven to 425°F. Generously grease an 8-inch cast-iron frying pan with an ovenproof handle with oil (a round cake pan can also be used). Place in the oven to heat while making the batter.

Sift the flour into a bowl, add the cornmeal and salt, and make a well in the center. Whisk together the egg, buttermilk, and oil, add to the dry ingredients, and stir until just combined. Be sure not to overbeat.

Spoon into the hot cast-iron pan or cake pan and bake for 25 minutes or until firm to the touch and golden brown. Cut into wedges and serve.

Makes 1 loaf

# Rosettas

2 teaspoons dried yeast

1 teaspoon sugar

4½ cups unbleached all-purpose
flour, sifted

1 teaspoon salt

3½ tablespoons butter, softened

¼ cup olive oil

1½ tablespoons superfine sugar

milk, to glaze

all-purpose flour, extra, to dust

Grease two baking trays. Place the yeast, sugar, and 1/2 cup warm water in a small bowl and stir well. Leave in a warm, draft-free place for 10 minutes or until bubbles appear on the surface. The mixture should be frothy and slightly increased in volume. If your yeast doesn't foam it is dead, so you will have to discard it and start again.

Set aside 1/4 cup of the flour and put the rest in a large bowl with the salt. Make a well in the center. Add the yeast mixture, butter, oil, sugar, and 1 1/4 cups warm water. Stir with a wooden spoon until the dough leaves the side of the bowl and forms a rough, sticky ball. Turn out onto a floured surface. Knead for 10 minutes or until the dough is smooth and elastic. Add enough of the reserved flour, if necessary, to make a smooth dough. Place in a large, lightly oiled bowl and brush the surface with melted butter or oil. Cover with plastic wrap and leave in a warm place for 1 hour or until well risen.

Punch down the dough, then knead for 1 minute. Divide into ten portions and shape each into a smooth ball. Place the balls 2 inches apart on the trays. Using a 1 1/4-inch round cutter, press a 1/2-inch-deep indent into the center of each ball. With a sharp knife, score five evenly spaced, 1/2-inch-deep cuts down the side of each roll. Cover with plastic wrap or a damp towel and leave in a warm place for 1 hour or until well risen.

Preheat the oven to 350°F. Brush the rolls with milk and sift a fine layer of the extra flour over them. Bake for 25 minutes or until golden. Rotate the trays in the oven if one tray is browning faster than the other. Cool on a rack.

Makes 10 rolls

Note: These are best eaten on the day they are baked, but can be frozen for up to 1 month.

# Beer bread

3 1/2 cups self-rising flour
1 teaspoon salt
1 teaspoon superfine sugar
1 teaspoon dill seeds
3 tablespoons butter, melted
1 1/2 cups beer
all-purpose flour, for kneading
dill seeds, extra
coarse sea salt

Preheat the oven to 375°F. Lightly grease a baking tray. Sift the flour and salt into a large bowl. Add the sugar and dill seeds and combine. Make a well in the center and add the butter and beer all at once. Using a wooden spoon, quickly mix to form a soft dough.

Turn out onto a floured surface, sprinkling extra flour on your hands and on the surface of the dough. Knead for 30–45 seconds. Elongate the ball slightly, flatten a little, and press down 3/4 inch along the center with the blunt end of a large knife. Brush the surface with water and sprinkle liberally with the extra dill seeds and sea salt.

Bake for 20 minutes, then reduce the oven to 350°F and bake for another 30 minutes or until the bread sounds hollow when tapped. Remove from the oven, place on a wire rack, and leave to cool.

Makes 1 loaf

Note: This bread is best eaten on the day of baking, but it freezes well for up to a week.

# Desserts

## Camembert with port-soaked raisins

2 tablespoons raisins
2 tablespoons port
12 oz. whole Camembert cheese
canola oil spray
almond bread, to serve

Put the raisins and port in a small saucepan over high heat until they just come to a boil, then allow the mixture to cool for about 30 minutes.

Cut a circular lid from the top of the Camembert, leaving a ¾-inch border. Carefully remove the lid and scoop out the soft cheese with a spoon, leaving the base intact. Put the raisins in the hole and top with the cheese, squashing it down so that as much as possible fits back into the cavity, then replace the lid.

Lightly spray a double layer of foil with canola spray and wrap the cheese to form a sealed package. Preheat a barbecue flat plate to low heat and cook the package for 8–10 minutes or until it is heated through and soft. Make sure the heat stays low, or the rind will become brown and burn. Serve with the almond bread.

Serves 4

Note: After cooking your main meal, there should be just enough heat left in the barbecue to warm the Camembert for this delicious dessert.

## Berry and marshmallow gratin

2 1/2 cups mixed seasonal berries
    (strawberries, raspberries,
    blueberries, blackberries) (see Note)
2 tablespoons raspberry liqueur
2 1/2 cups pink and white
    marshmallows
vanilla ice cream

Put the berries and raspberry liqueur in a bowl, stir them gently to coat the berries, and transfer them to a 6-cup ceramic ovenproof dish. Top the berries with the marshmallows, making sure they are evenly distributed over the surface.

Preheat a covered barbecue to medium–high indirect heat and put the dish in the middle of the barbecue. Cook for 8–10 minutes or until the berries are bubbling and the marshmallows have puffed up and are starting to melt. Serve the gratin immediately with a big scoop of ice cream, but be careful to not burn your mouth on the berries, which will be very hot.

Serves 6

Note: If it is not berry season and your berries are not as sweet as they should be, add a little superfine sugar with the liqueur. Use strawberries in a smaller proportion to the other berries, as they tend to release a lot of liquid.

# Grilled panettone with peaches

½ cup superfine sugar
½ vanilla bean, halved and scraped
1 tablespoon Grand Marnier
4 ripe peaches
vegetable oil, for brushing
4 large slices panettone
⅓ cup crème fraîche

Put the sugar, vanilla bean, and ¼ cup water in a small saucepan and stir over low heat until the sugar has dissolved. Simmer the mixture without stirring it for 10 minutes, then remove it from the heat, stir in the Grand Marnier, and keep it warm.

Dip the peaches into a saucepan of boiling water for 5 seconds, then rinse them under cold water and remove the skins, which should slip off easily. Cut the peaches in half, remove the pits, and lightly brush the cut sides with oil. Preheat a barbecue grill to medium heat and grill the peaches, cut-side down, for 5 minutes or until golden and warmed through. Grill the panettone for 30 seconds to 1 minute on each side or until it is marked and lightly toasted. The panettone will brown very quickly, so be careful not to burn it. Arrange the grilled peaches over the panettone, drizzle with the vanilla syrup, and serve with a scoop of crème fraîche.

Serves 4

# Pear and hazelnut crepes with cinnamon sugar

*Crepes*
2 cups all-purpose flour
3 eggs
1½ cups milk
4½ tablespoons butter, melted
melted butter, extra, for cooking

*Filling*
2 cups cream cheese
2 tablespoons confectioners'
  sugar, sifted
²/₃ cup hazelnuts, toasted, skinned,
  and roughly chopped
²/₃ cup candied peel
2 teaspoons finely grated lemon zest
2 tablespoons Frangelico or Poire
  William
1 large, firm green pear, cored and
  cut into ½-inch dice

2 tablespoons superfine sugar
1 teaspoon ground cinnamon

To make the crepe batter, sift the flour into a bowl with a pinch of salt and make a well. Gradually whisk in the combined eggs and milk until the batter is smooth, then stir in the melted butter. Strain the batter into a pitcher, cover, and refrigerate it for 1 hour. The consistency should be similar to thin cream, so add a little more milk if it looks too thick.

To make the filling, beat the cream cheese and confectioners' sugar in a bowl until smooth. Add the hazelnuts, peel, zest, and liqueur and stir it all together. Gently stir in the diced pear and refrigerate the filling until you are ready to use it.

Heat a 7-inch crepe or nonstick frying pan over low–medium heat and brush it with butter. Pour ¼ cup of batter into the pan and swirl it around so that the bottom of the pan is thinly covered. Cook the crepe for 1 minute or until the edges just begin to curl, then turn it over and cook the other side for 30 seconds. Slide the crepe out of the pan onto a plate and continue with the remaining batter, stacking the crepes as you go.

Put 2 heaping tablespoons of the filling in the middle of each crepe, fold two opposite sides in to the middle, and flatten the mixture slightly, then fold in the other two sides to enclose the filling.

Preheat a barbecue flat plate to low heat and cook the crepe wraps for 3–4 minutes on each side or until they are golden and crisp and the filling is warmed through. Transfer the crepes to serving plates, sprinkle with the combined superfine sugar and cinnamon, and serve immediately.

Makes 12 crepes

Note: If you are making the crepes in advance, stack them between sheets of waxed paper to keep them from sticking to each other. Do not refrigerate.

# Amaretti-stuffed apples with vanilla ricotta

2 tablespoons golden raisins
2 tablespoons amaretto
10 small amaretti cookies (about 2 1/4 oz.), crushed
2 tablespoons slivered almonds, toasted
1 tablespoon sugar
2 1/2 tablespoons butter, melted
4 Granny Smith apples

*Vanilla ricotta*
1/2 vanilla bean
2 tablespoons confectioners' sugar
1 cup ricotta cheese

Soak the raisins in the amaretto for 15 minutes or until they are softened, then add them to the crushed amaretti with the amaretto, slivered almonds, sugar, and 2 tablespoons of melted butter.

Scrape the seeds out of the vanilla bean and add them to the ricotta, along with the confectioners' sugar. Use an electric beater to beat the mixture until the ricotta is smooth and creamy.

Remove the apple cores and enough fruit from around the core to make a hole about 1 inch across. Stuff the hole with the amaretto mixture, brush the apples with the remaining melted butter, and wrap them securely in foil. Preheat a covered barbecue to low–medium indirect heat, put the apples on the barbecue, and cook them, covered, for 15–20 minutes or until they are tender. Serve with a big scoop of the vanilla ricotta.

Serves 4

Note: Vanilla ricotta is a delicious alternative to whipped cream to serve with desserts.

## Pineapple with brown sugar glaze and toasted coconut

1 pineapple
½ cup dark brown sugar
½ teaspoon vanilla extract
1 tablespoon Galliano
4½ tablespoons butter
2 tablespoons coconut flakes, toasted
vanilla ice cream

Peel the pineapple and remove all the "eyes," then slice it lengthwise into quarters and remove the core. Cut into long, ½-inch-wide wedges.

Put the brown sugar, vanilla extract, and 2 teaspoons water in a small saucepan and cook it over low–medium heat for 5 minutes or until the sugar has dissolved. Remove the pan from the heat, add the Galliano, then return the pan to the heat and simmer the mixture for 3 minutes. Whisk in the butter and continue to simmer the mixture over low heat for 15 minutes or until smooth and thick.

Preheat a barbecue grill to medium heat, brush the pineapple with the brown sugar glaze, and grill for 2–3 minutes or until grill marks appear. Arrange the pineapple pieces on a serving platter, top with the glaze and the toasted coconut, and serve with vanilla ice cream.

Serves 6

## Coconut pancakes with grilled bananas and syrup

$2/3$ cup brown sugar
2 tablespoons lime juice
1 cup all-purpose flour
$1/4$ cup rice flour
$1/2$ cup superfine sugar
$1/2$ cup dried coconut
2 cups coconut milk
2 eggs, lightly beaten
4 bananas, sliced thickly diagonally
2 tablespoons dark brown sugar
$3 1/2$ tablespoons butter, plus extra
  for cooking
$1/2$ cup shredded coconut, toasted
1 lime, cut into wedges

Put the brown sugar in a small, heavy-based saucepan with 1/2 cup water and stir it over low heat for 5 minutes or until the sugar has dissolved. Increase the heat to medium and let it simmer, without stirring, for 15 minutes or until the liquid becomes a thick, sticky syrup. Stir in the lime juice and keep the syrup warm.

Sift the flours together, add the superfine sugar and dried coconut, and stir it all together. Make a well in the middle and pour in the combined coconut milk and egg, beating until the mixture is smooth.

Preheat a barbecue flat plate to low–medium heat. Toss the bananas in the dark brown sugar and grill them around the cooler edges of the flat plate, dotting each piece with butter. Cook the banana, turning the pieces occasionally, for 4–5 minutes or until it begins to soften and brown. Melt a little of the extra butter in the middle of the plate and pour 1/4 cup of the pancake mixture on top, using the back of a spoon to spread it out to a 6-inch circle. Cook the pancake for 2–3 minutes or until the underside is golden, then turn it over and cook the other side for another minute. As each pancake is cooked, transfer it to a plate and cover it with a towel

to keep it warm. Add more butter to the flat plate as necessary and keep going until all of the pancake mixture has been used.

Fold each pancake into quarters and put two on each serving plate. Top with grilled banana, drizzle with a little brown sugar syrup, and sprinkle with the coconut. Serve with lime wedges.

Serves 4

## Fruit skewers with rum butter

1 peach, peeled, pitted, and cut
   into 8 pieces
1 mango, peeled, pitted, and cut
   into 8 pieces
8 strawberries, hulled and halved
1 lb. papaya, cut into 8 pieces
5½ oz. pineapple, cut into 8 pieces
2 bananas, cut into ¾-inch pieces
¾ cup dark rum
⅓ cup dark brown sugar
1 tablespoon butter
ice cream, to serve

Put the peach, mango, strawberries, papaya, pineapple, and banana in a bowl with the rum and sugar and stir gently until all of the fruit is coated in the marinade. Cover and refrigerate the bowl for 1 hour.

Soak eight wooden skewers in cold water for 1 hour. Drain the marinade into a small, heavy-based saucepan and thread the fruit onto the skewers. Make sure each skewer has a good mix of fruits and that the pieces are not crowded, otherwise they won't cook evenly.

Bring the marinade to a boil over medium heat, then reduce the heat and simmer for 5 minutes or until it is reduced and syrupy. Remove the pan from the heat and whisk in the butter until it becomes smooth and glossy.

Preheat a flat grill plate to medium heat and cook the skewers for 5–8 minutes on each side or until they are golden, basting them all over with the rum glaze during the last minute of cooking. Arrange the skewers on a serving plate, drizzle them with the rum glaze, and serve warm with ice cream.

Serves 4

# Basics

# Types of barbecues

There are two main methods of cooking on a barbecue. The first is to cook food over direct heat, such as over a wood fire or coal briquettes located directly under a grill or plate. The food must be turned during cooking so that it cooks evenly on both sides.

The other method is to use indirect heat, for which you need a barbecue with some kind of hood or cover. This method of cooking works a bit like an oven, by circulating the heat around the food, and it is mainly used for roasting larger cuts of meat, giving them a distinctive barbecue flavor.

## Wood-burning fixed barbecues are the traditional

backyard barbecue—usually a fairly simple model in the form of an elevated grill plate with a fire burning underneath. Although easy to use and available to anyone with the space, a few bricks, and a grill, the basic design lends itself only to fairly simple methods of cooking. Heat regulation is usually achieved by adjusting the fire and waiting for it to reach the right temperature, although it's preferable to let the flames die down and cook over a pile of glowing embers, which give off a more constant heat.

## Kettle barbecues are portable,

come in a range of sizes, and are designed for both direct and indirect cooking. A kettle barbecue has a rounded base, which holds barbecue fuel briquettes on a metal grill. If you want to cook with direct heat, simply grill the food over the coals. If you want to cook using the indirect method, arrange the briquettes in two piles on opposite sides of the bottom grill and put a drip tray between them before inserting the top grill. To give the heat a boost, open the vents in the outer shell of the barbecue—this will allow air to circulate, making the briquettes burn faster and hotter. To keep the temperature a little cooler, leave the vents closed.

## Gas barbecues are available in

a huge variety of sizes and shapes, from small portables to huge, wagon-style barbecues that come with a hood, rotisserie, and workbench on the side. They are convenient and simple to operate, usually requiring only 10 minutes or so to heat up and the turn of a knob to regulate temperature. Some work by means of a flame under the barbecue plate, while others use the flame to heat a bed of reusable volcanic rock. If your barbecue has a lid or hood, you can also cook using indirect heat.

**Electric barbecues** operate on a principle similar to that of gas barbecues, by heating the grill plate on which the food is cooked. They can be less convenient than a gas barbecue, as they require access to an electricity outlet and the heat produced may not be as even or as strong as that produced by a gas or coal barbecue.

## Methods of cooking

Indirect and direct heat are the main cooking methods when you are using a barbecue. Make sure you set up your barbecue properly to shorten cooking times and make sure that all your lovingly prepared meals are perfectly cooked.

## For direct cooking

Kettle barbecue: Start the barbecue and let the briquettes burn for about 45 minutes before you begin cooking. For a medium–hot setting, use about sixty briquettes; for a lower temperature, forty-five briquettes should be enough. If you need to lower the temperature when the fire is already set, just spritz the coals with a light spray of water, but if you want to increase the heat, you will need to add more briquettes and wait for the heat to develop.

Gas or electric barbecue: Light the barbecue and let it heat for about 10 minutes before cooking.

## For indirect cooking

Kettle barbecue: Start the barbecue (putting the fuel on each side to leave room for the drip tray) and leave the fire to develop for about 45 minutes. Put a drip tray between the coals and set the top grill in place. Position the food so that it is over the drip tray and cover it with the lid. Keep the bottom vents open so that the heat circulates evenly, and don't open the lid unless it's really necessary—the more often the heat is allowed to escape, the longer your cooking time will be.

Gas or electric barbecue: It's best to check the manufacturer's instructions on how to set up your barbecue for indirect cooking. In general, the outside burners are set to medium–low and the food sits in the middle of the barbecue. This means that the heat can circulate around the meat without burning it underneath.

# Barbecuing tips

• Food cooked on a grill plate can also be cooked on an open grill provided it is large enough to not fall through the holes.

• Food cooked on an open grill may also be cooked on a grill plate.

• Invest in a small fire extinguisher, in case of emergency.

• For best results, bring the meat to room temperature before cooking it, but it is not advisable to leave it sitting at room temperature for more than 20 minutes.

• Always make sure that your barbecue is clean before lighting it. If possible, clean it out as soon as it is cool enough, brushing or scraping the grill plates and discarding ash and embers.

• Assemble all the equipment you will need before you start cooking so that you won't have to leave the food unattended.

• Make sure that the barbecue is in a sheltered position and on a level surface, away from wooden fences, overhanging trees, or anything else that may be flammable.

• Brush or spray the barbecue with oil before lighting it in case the oil comes in contact with the flame and flares up. To keep food from sticking, brush it with oil just before cooking it, make sure the grill plate is the correct temperature, and don't turn the food until the surface of the food has cooked and released itself naturally from the grill.

• If you wish to use the marinade to baste, you must boil it, then let it simmer for at least 5 minutes before basting so that any bacteria from the raw meat are not transferred to the cooked meat.

• If you are basting the food with a sugary glaze, apply it only in the last 10 minutes of cooking, as it will tend to burn on the grill.

• Always soak wooden skewers for an hour before use to prevent them from charring on the grill.

• Salt meat just before barbecuing, as salt will quickly draw moisture out of the meat if it is left on too long.

# Cooking time guide

The cooking temperature in a kettle or covered barbecue is not always constant, so we've listed these times to use as a guide (500 g = 1 lb. 2 oz.).

## Beef per 500 g

| | with a bone | boneless |
| --- | --- | --- |
| rare | 15 minutes | 10 minutes |
| medium | 20 minutes | 15 minutes |
| well done | 25 minutes | 20 minutes |

## Leg of lamb per 500 g

| | |
| --- | --- |
| medium–rare | 10–15 minutes |
| medium | 20–25 minutes |
| well done | 30 minutes |

## Pork
Allow 30 minutes per 500 g.
Pork should be cooked through, but not overcooked or the flesh will be dry. Test that it is ready by inserting a skewer into the thickest part of the pork or close to the bone; the juices should be clear, with no trace of pink.

## Poultry
Allow 20–25 minutes per 500 g.
It's important that chicken is cooked right through with no pink flesh or juices inside. Check by inserting a skewer between the thigh and the body through to the bone; the juices should run clear.

## Fish
Allow 20–25 minutes per 500 g.
Different varieties of fish require different cooking times. Tuna and salmon steaks are often cooked medium–rare, as the flesh can become dry if cooked through. Depending on thickness, they may only need a few minutes on each side over direct heat. Most other fish are served cooked through. It is important to remove them from the barbecue as soon as they are ready, as residual heat in the flesh will continue to cook the meat. Test by inserting a thin-bladed knife into the thickest part of the fish; it will be ready when the flesh flakes cleanly.

# Glossary

**baste**  to spoon or brush cooking juices or other fat over food during cooking to keep it from drying out, or to help with heat transfer.

**brown**  to pan-fry, bake, grill, or roast food (often meat) so the outer surface turns a golden brown color.

**caramelize**  to cook until sugars, which either exist naturally in the food or are added (for example, in a marinade), become golden brown.

**charred**  when food is cooked on a grill until the surface is blackened.

**core**  to remove the core from fruit by using a corer or small knife.

**covered barbecue**  refers to a barbecue that has a fitted lid, which may be closed to make it suitable for roasting or slow cooking.

**dice**  to chop food into very small, even cubes. Use a very sharp knife to do this.

**drip tray**  used in kettle barbecues for indirect cooking. It is placed between the fuel briquettes to catch any dripping juices.

**dry-fry**  to cook spices in a dry frying pan until they become fragrant. Keep a close eye on spices cooked in this way, as they can burn quickly.

**fillet**  to cut the meat, fish, or poultry away from the bone. Also refers to the cut of meat, commonly taken from the top half of an animal's leg.

**flat grill plate**  a heavy, flat metal plate set over a heat source that doesn't allow the flames from the barbecue to actually touch the food. This means that there are no flare-ups caused by dripping juices or fat.

**glaze**  to coat food with a liquid as it is cooking. A glaze adds flavor, color, and shine.

**grease**  to lightly coat a pan or dish with oil or melted butter to prevent food from sticking.

**grill**  a heavy metal plate with slotted grill bars that allows the food to be directly exposed to the heat and fire below for a true barbecue flavor. It also refers to this method of cooking.

**heavy-based saucepan**
usually has a copper lining in the base, which allows for even and constant distribution of heat across the whole base of the pan.

**kettle barbecue**  refers to a rounded barbecue with a lid.

**marinate**  to tenderize and flavor food (usually meat) by leaving it in an acidulated, seasoned marinade.

**nonmetallic dish**  a ceramic or glass dish that will not react with any acids in the foods stored or marinated in it.

**parboil**  to partially cook a food in boiling water before some other form of cooking. Most commonly used for roast potatoes, which are parboiled before going into the roasting pan.

**puree**  food blended or processed to a pulp.

**reduce**  to boil or simmer liquid in an uncovered pan so that some of the liquid evaporates, causing the mixture to become thicker and the flavor more concentrated.

**rest**  to allow meat to sit, covered, for a period of time after it has cooked before slicing it. This enables the muscle fibers to relax and retain their juices when cut.

**rub**  a mixture of dried herbs and spices used as a dry marinade for foods, usually meat.

**score**  to make incisions with a knife (usually into fish or meat) in a crossed pattern, without cutting all the way through. This ensures even cooking through thicker sections of the food.

**shred**  to cut food into small, narrow strips, either by hand or using a grater or food processor with a shredding disk. Cooked meat may be shredded by pulling it apart with forks or your fingers.

**simmer**  to cook liquid, or food in a liquid, over low heat, just below boiling point. The surface of the liquid should be moving, with a few small bubbles coming to the surface.

**skim**  to remove fat or scum that comes to the surface of a liquid.

**smoke**  adding fragrant wood chips to the barbecue heat source to produce smoke that will impart a distinctive flavor to the food as it cooks. Works best with barbecue briquettes.

**strain**  to remove solids from a liquid by pouring it through a sieve. The solids are discarded, unless otherwise specified.

# Index

# Index

Adobo pork with coconut rice, 224
Amaretti-stuffed apples with vanilla
    ricotta, 376
Asian rice salad, 317
Asian salad, 345
asparagus, Grilled, 346
Avocado and grapefruit salad, 322

Baby spinach salad, 338
Bacon-wrapped chicken, 256
Barbecued baby potatoes, 349
Barbecued chermoula shrimp, 139
Barbecued corn on the cob, 314
Barbecued sardines, 175
Barbecued tuna and white bean salad, 267
Barbecue sauce, 329
beef
    with barbecue sauce, Roast, 264
    with blue-cheese butter, 184
    burgers, Chili, 47
    fajitas, 116
    kebabs with mint yogurt dressing, 10
    in lettuce leaves, Korean barbecue, 230
    and mozzarella burgers with grilled
        tomatoes, 55
    ribs with sweet potatoes, Bourbon-
        glazed, 146
    salad, Thai, 136
    Sesame and ginger, 215
Beer bread, 362
Berry and marshmallow gratin, 368
Blackened Cajun spiced chicken, 268
Bourbon-glazed beef ribs with sweet
    potatoes, 146
Brunch burgers with the works, 71
Bruschetta with mushrooms and mustard
    crème fraîche, 128

calamari with lime and chili dipping sauce,
    Stuffed baby, 279
Camembert with port-soaked raisins, 367
carrot salad, Moroccan spiced, 313
cauliflower salad with tahini dressing and
    gremolata, Grilled, 325

Cheeseburgers with red pepper salsa, 67
chicken
    Bacon-wrapped, 256
    Blackened Cajun spiced, 268
    burgers, Yakitori, 52
    Caesar salad, 187
    Five-spice roast, 211
    Honey mustard, 276
    with jasmine rice and Asian greens,
        Thai red, 102
    Lebanese, 196
    Lime and cilantro grilled, 164
    Margarita, 200
    Mirin and sake, 252
    with potato rosti, Thai spiced, 244
    Sage and ricotta stuffed, 76
    salad with arugula and cannellini beans, 84
    with salsa verde, 227
    Satay, 21
    skewers, Mediterranean, 42
    skewers, Persian, 33
    tikka with garlic naan and apple raita, 96
    wings, Crispy, 119
    with zucchini, Lemon and thyme roasted,
        134
Chickpea salad, 337
Chili bean tortilla wraps, 195
Chili beef burgers 47
Chili pork ribs, 171
Chinese barbecue pork with pancakes, 262
Chinese-style barbecue spareribs, 288
Chipolatas with cheese and jalapeño
    quesadillas, 87
Cilantro shrimp, 91
Coconut pancakes with grilled bananas
    and syrup, 382
coleslaw, Dill, 330
Corn bread, 357
corn on the cob, Barbecued, 314
crab with Singapore-style pepper sauce,
    Spicy, 163
Crispy chicken wings, 119
Crispy-skinned salmon salad niçoise, 156
Cucumber salad, 350

Damper, 354
Dill coleslaw, 330
Drumsticks in tomato and mango chutney, 236
duck breast with peach and chili salad, Spiced, 143

eggplant, Stuffed, 148
Eggplant, tomato, and sumac salad, 301

Fennel and pork sausages with onion relish, 280
Fennel salad, 309
Fillet steak with flavored butters, 271
fish, Vietnamese, 88
fish rosemary skewers with marjoram dressing and grilled radicchio salad, Scallop and, 22
Five-spice roast chicken, 211
Fruit skewers with rum butter, 384

Garlic and mint lamb skewers with almond couscous and yogurt sauce, 14
Ginger-orange pork, 124
Greek pepper lamb salad, 79
Grilled asparagus, 346
Grilled cauliflower salad with tahini dressing and gremolata, 325
Grilled haloumi salad, 172
Grilled mangoes, 298
Grilled panettone with peaches, 371
Grilled potatoes with pistachio salsa, 302
Grilled vegetables with basil aioli, 115
Guacamole, 334

haloumi salad, Grilled, 172
Herb burgers, 68
Hoisin lamb with charred scallions, 140
Honey mustard chicken, 276
Honey roasted pork fillet, 255

Involtini of swordfish, 17

Jumbo shrimp with dill mayonnaise, 183

Korean barbecue beef in lettuce leaves, 230

lamb
    burgers, 60
    with charred scallions, Hoisin, 140
    with chili aioli, Skewered, 34
    chops with citrus pockets, 208
    cutlets with mint gremolata, 127
    cutlets with orange sweet potatoes and ginger nori butter, Marinated, 94
    fillets with baba ghanoush, Sumac-crusted, 104
    fillets wrapped in vine leaves with avgolemono sauce, 190
    on grilled polenta with anchovy sauce, Rosemary, 284
    kebabs with skordalia, Paprika, 25
    kofta with baba ghanoush and grilled olives, 220
    Marinated, 259
    Roast, 176
    salad, Greek pepper, 79
    skewers with almond couscous and yogurt sauce, Garlic and mint, 14
    souvlaki roll, 160
    stuffed with olives, feta, and oregano, 168
    with tomato and onion salsa, Tandoori, 235
Lebanese chicken, 196
Lemon and sage marinated veal chops with arugula, 287
Lemon and thyme roasted chicken with zucchini, 134
Lime and cilantro grilled chicken, 164
Lobster with burned butter sauce and grilled lemon, 216

Malaysian barbecued seafood, 152
mangoes, Grilled, 298
Margarita chicken, 200
Marinated lamb, 259
Marinated lamb cutlets with orange sweet potatoes and ginger nori butter, 94
Marinated vegetable salad with bocconcini and pesto dressing, 243

# Index

Mashed potatoes with scallions, 310
Mediterranean chicken skewers, 42
Minted potato salad, 326
Mirin and sake chicken, 252
Miso-glazed salmon and eggplant salad
    with sesame dressing, 131
Moroccan spiced carrot salad, 313
Moroccan squash on pistachio couscous, 82
Mushroom and eggplant skewers with
    tomato sauce, 37
mushroom salad, Warm marinated, 333

octopus, Sweet chili, 212
octopus, Teriyaki baby, 292

Paprika lamb kebabs with skordalia, 25
Parsley carrots, 341
Pear and hazelnut crepes with cinnamon
    sugar, 374
Pear and walnut salad, 297
Pepper steaks with horseradish sauce, 99
Persian chicken skewers, 33
Pineapple with brown sugar glaze and
    toasted coconut, 379
Pineapple mint salsa, 318
Piri piri shrimp, 112
pork
    with apple and onion wedges, 199
    chops with grilled scallions, Stuffed, 180
    with chunky applesauce and vegetables,
        Roast rack of, 274
    with coconut rice, Adobo, 224
    fillet, Honey roasted, 255
    Ginger-orange, 124
    kebabs, Sweet-and-sour, 18
    kebabs with garlic sauce, Spice-rubbed, 30
    loin with apple glaze and potato wedges, 159
    with pancakes, Chinese barbecue, 262
    ribs, Chili, 171
    sausage burgers with mustard cream, 56
    sausages with onion relish, Fennel and, 280
    skewers in green ginger wine and soy
        marinade with grilled scallions, 9
    and tomato burgers, 51

Portuguese spatchcock, 108
potatoes, Barbecued baby, 349
potatoes with pistachio salsa, Grilled, 302
potato salad, Minted, 326

Ratatouille, 353
Red pepper relish, 321
rice salad, Asian, 317
Roast beef with barbecue sauce, 264
Roast lamb, 176
Roast rack of pork with chunky applesauce
    and vegetables, 274
Roast sirloin with mustard pepper crust and
    hasselback potatoes, 250
Rosemary lamb on grilled polenta with
    anchovy sauce, 284
Rosemary and red wine steaks with
    barbecued vegetables, 203
Rosettas, 360

Sage and ricotta stuffed chicken, 76
salmon and eggplant salad with sesame
    dressing, Miso-glazed, 131
salmon salad niçoise, Crispy-skinned, 156
Salmon and shrimp kebabs with Chinese
    spices, 41
sardines, Barbecued, 175
Satay chicken, 21
Scallop and fish rosemary skewers with
    marjoram dressing and grilled radicchio
    salad, 22
Scallops with sesame bok choy, 192
seafood, Malaysian barbecued, 152
seafood salad with romesco sauce,
    Spanish-style, 206
Sesame and ginger beef, 215
shrimp
    Barbecued chermoula, 139
    Cilantro, 91
    with dill mayonnaise, Jumbo, 183
    kebabs with Chinese spices, Salmon
        and, 41
    Piri piri, 112
Skewered lamb with chili aioli, 34

Smoked trout with lemon and dill butter, 240

Smoky tomato sauce, 306

Snapper envelope with ginger and scallions, 122

Spanish-style seafood salad with romesco sauce, 206

spareribs, Chinese-style barbecue, 288

spatchcock, Portuguese, 108

Spiced duck breast with peach and chili salad, 143

Spice-rubbed pork kebabs with garlic sauce, 30

Spicy buffalo wings with ranch dressing, 223

Spicy crab with Singapore-style pepper sauce, 163

squash on pistachio couscous, Moroccan, 82

Squid with picada dressing, 232

Steak sandwich with balsamic onions and sun-dried tomato and basil cream, 63

Stuffed baby calamari with lime and chili dipping sauce, 279

Stuffed eggplant, 148

Stuffed pork chops with grilled scallions, 180

Sumac-crusted lamb fillets with baba ghanoush, 104

Sweet chili octopus, 212

Sweet-and-sour pork kebabs, 18

swordfish, Involtini of, 17

Swordfish with tomato butter and grilled asparagus, 75

Tabbouleh, 305

Tandoori lamb with tomato and onion salsa, 235

Teriyaki baby octopus, 292

Thai beef salad, 136

Thai red chicken with jasmine rice and Asian greens, 102

Thai spiced chicken with potato rosti, 244

Tofu kebabs with miso pesto, 13

Tomato salsa, 342

trout with lemon and dill butter, Smoked, 240

tuna

burgers with herbed mayonnaise, 48

skewers with Moroccan spices and chermoula, 26

steaks on cilantro noodles, 247

steaks with salsa and garlic mashed potatoes, 151

and white bean salad, Barbecued, 267

veal chops with arugula, Lemon and sage marinated, 287

Veal steaks with caper butter, 107

Vegetarian burgers with cilantro garlic cream, 64

Vegetarian skewers with basil couscous, 38

Vietnamese fish, 88

Warm marinated mushroom salad, 333

Yakitori chicken burgers, 52

Recipe Writers: Vanessa Broadfoot, Ross Dobson, Kathleen Gandy, Jane Lawson, Christine Osmond, Rebecca Truda.

Special thanks to MUD Australia, Major & Tom, and Kif Kaf Designs, who supplied props and accessories for photography, and Woodland Home Products Pty Ltd and Weber Australia for providing the barbecues.

**Laurel Glen Publishing**
An imprint of the Advantage Publishers Group
5880 Oberlin Drive, San Diego, CA 92121-4794
www.laurelglenbooks.com

All notations of errors or omissions should be addressed to Laurel Glen Publishing, Editorial Department, at the above address. All other correspondence (author inquiries, permissions, and rights) concerning the content of this book should be addressed to Murdoch Books Pty Limited Australia, GPO Box 4115, Sydney NSW 2001, Australia.

NOTE: Those who might be at risk from the effects of salmonella poisoning (the elderly, pregnant women, young children, and those with a compromised immune system) should consult their physician before trying recipes made with raw eggs.

Library of Congress Cataloging-in-Publication Data:
BBQ food.
p. cm.
ISBN 1-59223-274-4
1. Barbecue cookery. I. Laurel Glen Publishing.
TX840.B3B376 2004
641.5'784--dc22
2004047260

Printed by Sing Cheong Printing Co. Ltd, Hong Kong
1 2 3 4 5   08 07 06 05 04

Editorial Director: Diana Hill
Editor: Rachel Carter
Creative Director: Marylouise Brammer
Designer: Michelle Cutler
Photographers: Alan Benson, Ian Hofstetter
Stylists: Jane Hann, Katy Holder
Food Preparation: Vanessa Broadfoot, Jo Glynn
Production: Fiona Byrne
Picture Librarian: Anne Ferrier
Chief Executive: Juliet Rogers
Publisher: Kay Scarlett

You may find cooking times vary depending on the oven you are using. For convection ovens, as a general rule, set the oven temperature 40°F lower than indicated in the recipe.
We have used large eggs in all recipes.